THE EARLY DAYS OF ESPN

The Early Days of ESPN

300 Daydreams and Nightmares

Peter Fox

LYONS
PRESS

Essex, Connecticut

LYONS PRESS

An imprint of Globe Pequot, the trade division of
The Rowman & Littlefield Publishing Group, Inc.
4501 Forbes Blvd., Ste. 200
Lanham, MD 20706
www.rowman.com

Distributed by NATIONAL BOOK NETWORK

British Library Cataloguing in Publication Information available

Library of Congress Cataloging-in-Publication Data
Names: Fox, Peter, 1942– author.
Title: The early days of ESPN : 300 daydreams and nightmares / [Peter Fox].
Other titles: Early days of Entertainment and Sports Programming Network
Description: Essex, Connecticut : Lyons Press, [2024] | Summary: "The story of the early days at
    ESPN, told by one of its founders, and how a conversation over a couple of martinis in 1978 led
    to the creation of a broadcast juggernaut"— Provided by publisher.
Identifiers: LCCN 2023050397 (print) | LCCN 2023050398 (ebook) | ISBN 9781493079575
    (cloth : alk. paper) | ISBN 9781493079582 (electronic)
Subjects: LCSH: ESPN (Television network)—History. | Television broadcasting of sports—
    History.
Classification: LCC GV742.3 .F69 2024 (print) | LCC GV742.3 (ebook) | DDC 384.55/540973-
    -dc23/eng/20231201
LC record available at https://lccn.loc.gov/2023050397
LC ebook record available at https://lccn.loc.gov/2023050398

♾️™ The paper used in this publication meets the minimum requirements of American National
Standard for Information Sciences—Permanence of Paper for Printed Library Materials, ANSI/
NISO Z39.48-1992.

INSPIRATION

I call us 'SPNauts.

We are ESPN's founding worker bees.

Our stories are worth telling.

So we did.

And then sports fans everywhere

Became our ground control.

Contents

Contents

Foreword by Bill Rasmussen

Garry Swain's overtime shorthanded goal christened professional hockey in Hartford Connecticut's Civic Center as Bob Neumeier and I broadcast the Hartford Whalers' victory in front of a sold-out crowd of 10,507 fans on January 11, 1975.

That was also the night I met Peter Fox, now the author of *The Early Days of ESPN: 300 Daydreams and Nightmares*.

In the hubbub that followed Swain's heroics, Peter showed up at our broadcast position, sticking out an introductory hand and saying, "We need to become friends."

We connected, he no shrinking violet, and me, an unrelenting gusher of to-do lists. We became fast friends, golfing, and even coproducing Greater Hartford Open PGA Tour radio broadcasts before ESPN was even an inkling.

When it was time to put flesh on the skinny ESP Network frame, it was he and a cast of other talented dreamers who became the 'SPNauts buckled onto a sports broadcasting rocket. It's those very earliest contributors to the vision that *The Early Days of ESPN* thoroughly, rightfully, and finally salutes.

So much has been written about the immense influence ESPN has had on the world of sports. Yet, few have celebrated the ingenuity of the band of risk-taking doulas, accoucheurs, and midwives who birthed the network.

The souls in repose of spirits like Bob Hempstead, Esq., Guy Wilson, Bob Bray, Ed McMahon's son Mike, and our first and wonderful voice, Lou Palmer, echo through the pages in stories told of them by peers, and in some cases their children.

Architect Geoff Bray thrills the reader with original pencil drawings of ESPN's first studio, while former *Hartford Times* sports editor Dennis Randall, who became our original PR director, digs deep into his archives to unearth his optimistic press releases.

Some of those 'SPNauts write their versions of how they felt when overrun by big money and how they feel about their role 40-plus years later.

As I write this I think of influencers without whom the dream would have faltered: University of Connecticut athletic director John Toner shepherded our very earliest introduction to NCAA; United Cable's Jim Dovey made his offices—even his attic—available to our network obstetric team; Budweiser's Mike Roarty and his ad agency exec Gene Petrillo unlocked ad budgets that attracted financiers.

For me a *The Early Days of ESPN* cherry-on-top is the retrospective written by renowned *New York Times* reviewer Bryan Miller, who as a rookie reporter, in 1979, scooped the rest of the sports media with a 3,000-word article under a cover that read "Why Are ABC, CBS and NBC Afraid of This Man?"

'SPNauts were pioneers. Their kids are proud. But the crowing belongs to their grandchildren. Thanks to this book, 'SPNaut grandkids get to brag about their grandparents who changed sports forever.

Bill Rasmussen was a cofounder of ESPN and its first president and CEO.

Foreword by Barbara Bodnar

To call Peter Fox a word artist is an understatement. He is a word therapist. He writes in a way that reaches deep into your soul with every word.

Give him a pen. Ask him for a word or two. Share your thoughts and Peter magic begins.

Once his fingers dance across a keyboard, products, jobs, or business ventures take on a special personality of their own.

From his earliest days as a journalist and speechwriter and avid sportsman, he turned images and feelings into a story or a profile, an idea into a sensation.

When he tackled an advertising challenge, success followed.

Need a political speech to change hearts and minds? Find Peter.

Turn sports news into inspiration? That's him again.

Give him a germ of an idea for a new venture and the magic erupts.

His latest adventure explores the stories of other often unheralded sports pioneers. He's curated a road map of what it takes to pull together the people, the ideas, and the call to disrupt.

The Peter Fox story involves struggles, culture and talent, serious hurdles, and giant leaps of faith, and his creations are his legacy.

It winds its way from hick to hero in the canyons of enterprise; *The Early Days of ESPN* recounts the network's earliest days and becomes an artifact in a life of loving what you do and doing it well.

Ms. Bodnar and Peter Fox have been friends, business partners, competitors, and mutual cheerleaders since her days as a Top 40 radio creative director and his as a political speechwriter.

Preface

During the 25th anniversary of ESPN's frequently publicized first tele-cast of 7 p.m. on September 7, 1979, I wrote an article in *Connecticut Magazine* that carried a "Before the Before" headline chronicling the November 17, 1978, actual first telecast of the fledgling network.

I agree to all pickers of nits that we were then known as ESP Net-work, but c'mon.

We televised sports programming from that first basketball game, through the gymnastic, track and field and baseball seasons intermit-tently, while we missionaried the all-sports religion to cable television moguls around the country during the 300 days before the second first ESPN telecast.

The point I made weakly then was that a makeshift tribe of pioneers, freelancers, and flat-out sports nuts managed to televise a series of Uni-versity of Connecticut sports on the only satellite in the sky that allowed commercial television.

In the ensuing time I came to understand the value those local folks brought to the revolution of television sports. It was an incredible time in the late 1970s and early 1980s when brashly, boldly, and perhaps a bit blindly we did cause big-time puckering in the sports television c-suites.

I would also posit that our lightning-fast acceptance begat a viewing revolution birthing other network verticals that comprise a litany that begins with news, music, food, sex, religions, et al.

It is for those brash and bold early 'SPNauts that this work is aggregated.

As you'll see, it weaves memories of mine, clear and clouded, and paraphrased from notes of interviews with key personalities.

You'll read actual quotes from taped interviews.

And for me the most interesting parts are the italicized in-their-own-words stories by colleagues and friends who have agreed that the rocket we rode left indelible memories, and even a scar or two.

I invited as many 'SPNauts as I could aggregate and am grateful for those who participated and understand those who elected to remain comfortable in their quiet.

To your and my never-ending pleasure were contributed images and artifacts foraged from musty cabinets and dusty attics.

Many of us are in repose, and many of our progeny have little or no knowledge of how big a contribution their parents or grandparents made to disrupting, improving, and certainly revolutionizing televised sports ESPN presents to sports fans everywhere, all day and every day.

We shared an extraordinary accomplishment, and our daydreams and nightmares needed telling, before they totally dissolved into the ether.

PROLOGUE

In tribute to the disruption of televised sports that ESPN dreamers wrought, this prologue disrupts a storytelling norm by placing the happy ending right smack in the beginning.

Let me bring you there in the words of ESPN founder William R. Rasmussen, my friend, who recollected the dramatic moment his dream and the dream of fellow early 'SPNauts came true in his book *Sports Junkies Rejoice*.

SEPTEMBER 7, 1979, 6:58 P.M.
ESPN Launch Minus Two Minutes

"Two minutes to launch," says the timekeeper.

Director Bill Creasy orders, "Everybody not involved in the opening show, please leave the studio."

"Ninety seconds to launch," says the timekeeper.

Nervous fingers check, check, and reset settings on camera control units, VTRs, audio levels, uplink levels, and on and on.

SEPTEMBER 7, 1979, 6:59 P.M.
Launch Minus One Minute

The director takes over: "One minute to air. Looking good, Lee stand by! VTR?"

"VTR, OK."

"Audio?"

"Audio, check."

"Satellite?"

"Video and audio confirmed by Vernon Valley."

"Thirty seconds to air. Stand by in studio."

"Stand by audio theme cart."

"Camera One, a little tighter please, we open with you."

"Lee take your cue for the AD next to Camera One. We can't get the IFB communications to your headset."

Lee nods.

"Twenty seconds."

Sweaty palms for several of us in the control room. I can't decide whether the second hand is moving too fast or too slow. *The tension is immense*. No more nervous conversation. We're all transfixed by the scene on the other side of the glass . . .

"Ten seconds."

"Stand by to roll theme."

"Stand by Camera One. Good luck everybody."

Anxious 'SPNauts on the control room side of the *SportsCenter* studio glass transfixed in the moments before the launch of ESPN at 7:00 p.m., September 7, 1979. Author Peter Fox in the center mirrors the intensity of colleagues Jim Rosenberg and Ellen Beckwith in the foreground, and left to right in the back row, Bob Waller, Jules Wynn, John Foley, Barry Black, Joe Gianquinto, and Scott Rasmussen.
PHOTO COURTESY ESPN

"Five seconds to air, Lee."

"Three."

"Two."

"One."

SEPTEMBER 7, 1979, 7:00 P.M.

ESPN Launch

"Take one and roll theme."

"Theme under . . . and cue Lee."

"If you love sports . . . if you really love sports, you'll think you've died and gone to sports heaven."

An indelible moment for the men and women who built ESPN. The earliest of 'SPNauts and the adrenaline-fueled months prior to the day sports got a new power are the subject of *The Early Days of ESPN*, answering the oft-asked question: "Do you think all-sports television will work?" An easy *yes!* falls off my lips when golfing buddy and eventual ESPN founder Bill Rasmussen invites me to become the founding executive producer of the ESPN dream.

Nearly five decades later, to square the table I'm spilling kudos over some, and vinegar and single malts on others who were part of the 300 days that came before ESPN made headlines and became the subject of a thick library of tomes written by journalists who weren't there.

Much glorified, and rightfully so, are the moments at seven o'clock on the evening of September 7 in 1979, when RCA Satellite Satcom 1 began receiving full-time signals from a veritable Skunk Works of television that was ESPN's sign-on studio, not yet weather sealed.

Those moments serve as the end to *The Early Days of ESPN*. The beginning builds around relationships personal, professional, and productive and starts well before the 300 days identified as the story's start, though for symmetry it is pinned to the day Lou Palmer and I went on ESPN payroll—300 days before full-time sign-on.

Days later, a ragtag band of 'SPNauts tossed a signal into the stars, also at seven o'clock, but on November 17, 1978, the network's first actual telecast, a preseason basketball game between the University of Connecticut and the barnstorming Bible-ballers Athletes in Action.

Founder Rasmussen and I had a personal, professional, long-standing, and continuing chemistry that Bill recounts in his foreword. The ESPN daydreaming and sometime nightmaring began when Bill asked me the all-sports-television question over dinner at landmark Cooke's Tavern, a mailman's saunter from ESPN's birth home at 319 Cooke Street, in Plainville, Connecticut, then home to a United Cable Television branch.

Two future-fuel-vermouth-splashed-see-thrus, and it was game's on!

Mayhem, swashbuckling, and risk-wrangling by a cadre of other buddies, colleagues, and money movers combined to make one of the most momentous modern stories in media.

Years of spending millions of advertising client dollars with broadcast properties in Connecticut allowed me to develop great relationships with Connecticut talents who ultimately became 'SPNauts. It is to these men and women who in less than a year took ESPN's shifting sportsworld concept—developed by father and son, stuck in a traffic jam—from scribbles to dribbles, homers, goals, touchdowns, and, yes, the agony of defeat in less than a year.

For sure there are after-stars that the network's PR machine duly acknowledged, yet this effort is meant to spotlight the souls of ESPN, its 1978 and 1979 grunts, all talented and in a way brave.

The back end of the 300 days got very exciting and personally stressful. The fun and stress days were divided by money. When big money made ESPN real, the strings attached added nightmares to the first wave of visionaries, friends, and earliest joiners, many of whom are invited to tell their stories, excerpted here.

How in the world did hicks-from-the-sticks ever get Getty Oil to open its purse strings to finance round-the-clock sports? This story is told in detail by a last-man-standing Getty guy whose pride is evidenced in an essay offered within.

"Hicks-from-the-sticks" was the slur aimed at us by a posse of sycophants to the cavalry of big-time TV executives that Getty's financial lube recruited. Or was it insensitive graffiti posted in an under-construction porta-potty? Either way, it was a stake to the heart of the earliest builders and an undercurrent that never went away.

So much has been written about the success and influence of ESPN on global sports, most of which is in its afterbirth. The stories in this book are prenatal, in unheralded voices remembered or spoken by the 'SPNauts who were sometimes flying blind toward a vision and a dream.

It was actually 200 days short of 9/7/79 when the Getty gusher splayed dollars in directions that forever changed the face of sports television, and another 100 days before the NBC cavalry arrived to plumbline ESPN's straight-ahead, take yes for all answers or get out of its rocket-riding way.

Collected, curated, sprinkled throughout, and narrated are play-by-plays, highlights, and docu-tattles by the likes of Chris Berman, local weather broadcaster; Scott Rasmussen, cofounder, son of Bill, cum political pollster; Bob Pronovost, swashbuckling roommate, and *SportsCenter* director; and Stuart Evey, Getty's Darth Vader who oiled the dream with money. You'll meet an original investor who forked over initial running money, not because he was turned on to sports, but because he'd worked with high tech while in the Marine Corps. You'll read a written-today story by the rookie newspaperman who scooped the world with the original ESPN story.

See the actual pencil sketches of ESPN's original broadcast studio and read the handwritten directions to the architect. Understand the serendipity that inevitably accompanies right-place-at-the-right-time phenomena and the wisdom to harness good fortune when it smacks you in the face mask.

Marvel at pre-cell, almost pre-fax, and certainly pre-laptop, internet, and artificial intelligence cotton-eared entrepreneurs and sports believers who knew in their bellies sports fans would gorge on round-the-clock sports television.

Find an affinity for some early ESPN-aligned organizations that took risks, too. The University of Connecticut and its athletic department lead the way.

Feel the joy and pride of living 'SPNauts and hear the voices of some in repose. Families are formed and dissolved. Careers blossom. Generations iterate.

Face the demons of a pair of high-functioning drunks, whose rivalry during those ever-so-stressful birthing days is marked by binges and badass bumfuckery. Follow the angels who, before the story ends, bring them peace and sobriety.

Yes, all-sports television worked. The unheralded men and women who knew it could finally get to share pride, jubilation, and "I told you so" moments in *The Early Days of ESPN*.

That indelible, incredible moment, seven o'clock in the evening of September 7, 1979, changed sports and television forever.

CHAPTER I

Who Knew?

THE ECHO OF THE QUESTION *DO YOU THINK ALL-SPORTS TELEVISION WILL work?* may appear ad nauseam as we work our way through ESPN's earliest days. Those who'll be recalled here will be the personalities who without folderol encouraged all-sports round-the-clock television during the idea's pregnancy.

There's much about founder Bill Rasmussen, and I'll leave the recounting of his good works to others. Bill's foreword to this book speaks to our relationship. Undoubtedly he changed sports television and sports itself.

The author of the September 1979 *Connecticut Magazine* article posing Bill mischievously on its cover asking rhetorically why the bigs were wetting their skivvies was rookie journalist Bryan Miller, who penned the first real ESPN shocker story. We printed, reprinted, and reprinted it again and passed it about the media marketplace with an equally mischievous glee, igniting a PR firestorm.

Miller, then just out of college and later a renowned *New York Times* restaurant reviewer and author, through a 30-plus-year lens recounts the experience:

> *Shortly out of college, at my second journalism gig, I lived in a creaky old barn—not a cutely renovated barn, but a working barn that retained heat like a screen door. I did not watch much television because my rabbit ears antenna had a reception range roughly equal to a first down. Cable was*

CONNECTICUT MAGAZINE, SEPTEMBER 1979

growing fast but had not yet snaked its way to the backwoods of Easton, Connecticut.

One day in the office I was leafing through a trade magazine that covered the broadcasting industry—I can't remember why I subscribed to it—and spotted a three-paragraph story about a broadcasting outfit in, of all places, Bristol, a moribund industrial town southwest of Hartford. The brief said something about satellites and cable and 24 hours of sports. Sounded like something worth checking out.

I drove up to the modest office of a company called ESPN and met with the genial founder named William Rasmussen, who for years had been involved in regional sports broadcasting. I was ill prepared for what I presumed would be a half-hour chat and a 300-word story. I remained for the afternoon and eventually wrote more than 3,000 words about what would become nothing short of a revolution in sports television.

Rasmussen had a laid back, disarming way about him and a knack for making complex subjects understandable. There was no hype, no bravado.

That first interview was a cutting-edge primer on satellites and transponders, and cable television (ironically, Connecticut was the last state in the US to receive cable, in 1971). On the second visit Rasmussen explained the business side of his ambitious project. For a man going way out on a million-dollar limb, he was as cool and confident as a riverboat gambler.

"I knew I had a sellable idea," he said. "And I figured the financing would come from somewhere." And it did. And Connecticut Magazine *scooped everybody, even the* New York Times. *And it wasn't long before I could sate my appetite for UConn women's volleyball.*

BEFORE THE BEFORE

Television for me was a siren, calling and calling and calling. And sports led me to it.

Before Dad brought our first television home, I'd watch flickering images in a peeping tom way on tiptoes peering through the living room window of the Couture family, who owned the first radio with pictures on our street.

I remember running from grammar school in September of 1954 to the home of my Aunt Jacqueline and Uncle Jack, who'd splurged on a television to, out of breath, see with my own eyes the blast by Vic Wertz to deep center field of the Giants' Polo Grounds, where Willie Mays proceeded to make the history with "The Catch," an over-the-shoulder snare.

Because I came from a large family and knew my way around a diaper and infant feeding, I was in demand as a babysitter locally. A working television was a requirement for my services.

Growing out of the newspaper business, for a spell I worked marketing banking services and spent time ghosting the speechifying of politicians.

It was during this period that I met a man whose life story influenced mine.

Aldo De Dominicus

When I met Aldo he was the epitome of the old-country elder, having turned over many of his media properties to his nephew Enzo, who put some contemporary touches to the marketing of a pair of Hartford radio stations he managed. Enzo would stage an annual show-off fest for advertising buyers, and we'd all put on airs and congregate in what for me was a must-go open bar and oyster and beef luncheon. It was there that Aldo held court, reaching across his head table centered seat to nod in a Marlon Brando way. The more temperate would dine and lie about their new clients and go back to work.

Not me, and I got to sit in a vacated chair next to Aldo and ask him how he came to build WNHC Channel 6, Connecticut's first television station. Aldo's English is heavily accented, but through it I heard him tell of selling pasta when he came to America. You get the gist.

And then, in an allusion to an appliance business, Aldo said it was hard to sell televisions where there was nothing for people to watch. *Bingo!* Feeding the sports and television tapeworm was to be like selling refrigerators to replace the iceman. Thank you, Aldo and Enzo.

Later, during my off Madison Avenue days, the question of sports and television came from the mouth of a client with an entrepreneurial spirit.

Bob Gruskay

Years before ESPN a client of mine, WPOP Radio general manager Robert Gruskay, was considering the purchase of a failing UHF television station based in Hartford, Connecticut, Channel 18, and asked me if all-sports programming would work.

Channel 18 began as an RKO pay-per-view experiment and when that failed, migrated to an all-Jesus-all-the-time format, but was eventually put up for sale. Gruskay knew the Connecticut sports fan had a voracious appetite and not much to assuage it, locally. He also knew that Boston and New York sports teams had a harmonic convergence over Connecticut but with no regular viewing source.

I knew it in my bones, having spent thousands of hours as a kid listening to the likes of Mel Allen, Curt Gowdy, Marty Glickman, Les Keiter, Johnny Most, and Red Barber call baseball and basketball games with my paper-route-financed transistor radio sequestered under my pillow after lights out.

Bob Gruskay's purchase of Channel 18 never materialized, but the thinking that went into his question set me up for the same query years later when Bill Rasmussen asked it again.

Gruskay in a way was responsible for my professional relationship with Rasmussen and later, by way of introduction, the pirating of WPOP's creative director as a business partner. I had negotiated the rights to radio broadcast PGA Tour's Sammy Davis Jr. Greater Hartford Open and needed an experienced voice to complement my golfing mentor and historian Jack Burrill. Enter Bill Rasmussen again.

While I produced and Jack and Bill broadcast on-the-half-hour highlights from Hartford's big-league event, we provided WPOP a sports product fully sponsored by Hamilton Beach, the then-Connecticut-based small appliance manufacturer.

ORIGINAL 'SPNAUTS

The intent here is to shine moments of acknowledgment on folks whose intuition told them the concept had promise and all-sports television would work!

Bill's son Scott did not receive much ink in press accounts of ESPN's rise, though his entrepreneurial skill revealed itself later when he founded a successful polling company.

There's little on record about the late Ed Eagan's founding role and his Getty-induced early exit, though I remember him, one cowboy boot lounging on an early desk, accompanied by an endless toothy smile.

As founders, Scott and Ed deserve a little more than a dismissive sentence. They played an undeniable role in the insemination of ESP-TV, the embryonic iteration of the current sports media behemoth.

Those pioneering personalities were joined by Dennis Randall and Vivian Arsego, who supported the dream as the card-carrying original believers.

We were also supported by a United Cable Television team led by Jim Dovey and Eric Hansen, who invited us into their Plainville, Connecticut, offices to work the dream. Add J. B. Doherty, the satellite-savvy money man who found the Getty gold mine for us and invested in our first-flight rickety rocket.

Scott Rasmussen

The Rasmussens were the public envy of many would-be father-son business tandems. Scott served to temper Bill's energetic vision. He could work a spreadsheet, while Bill's sheets served as sails into unknown media waters.

Taking an early parachute from the ESPN rocket ride, I watched Scott make a fundamental marketing mistake by trying to reprise all-sports broadcasting in radio.

Simply, ESPN went to cable operators capable of distributing hundreds of channels and pitched to be included. Scott's Enterprise Radio went to existing radio stations and in effect, said the all-sports programming should replace the programming already in place and on air.

In what is Rasmussen resilience, he has gone on to reinvent himself a few times, building and then divesting from the widely recognized Rasmussen Reports, a political, business, and lifestyle thermometer on trends and opinions in America. He continued to innovate in that space with ScottRasmussen.com and RMG Research.

In his inimitable succinct way, in a recent conversation with Scott he capsulized the ESPN eruption with this gem: "another reason it succeeded is we were too stupid to know it couldn't be done!"

Ed Eagan Jr.

Ed Eagan Jr. was founding principal and vice president of ESP-TV, an insurance agent by profession, and a TV producer/programmer by passion. His role in ESPN's birthing is significant, though he was the first casualty of Getty Oil's swatting of homegrown talent.

In an irony far from understandable, he is reported to have said he "took one for the team" when Getty bully and pending money gusher Stu Evey was said to say "either Eagan is out or the deal is off," during last-minute acquisition negotiations.

He went on to reprise his community television role that began with United Cable in Connecticut in Ludlow, Vermont, where he served as Chamber of Commerce executive director for many years.

In a perfect illustration of his quirky promotional acumen, as an attention-getting stunt for the expanded Okemo Valley tourist destination, Eagan created the Okemo Valley Zuccapult Competition, an air cannon shooting of zucchinis event. Eagan continued his community television involvement there, coupling his love for fishing with a pilot program *Let's Fish, Let's Catch*, before passing in 2009.

Don Rasmussen

Don is Bill's brother and is author of *Just a Guy, An Autobiography of the Quiet Founder of ESPN*. In it he recounts early ESPN investments of his own and other family members. He also raves of his experiences acting as the network's Midwest marketing manager, recounting his pride in personally bringing over 3 million subscribers to the network in its earliest days.

As can happen with family retellings of events, the Rasmussen family's versions of investments are not mirrored in their telling. I haven't met Don, so I will defer to his colleague Jim Bates, who held a similar post in the Northeast, to speak of him.

> *It would be a "dereliction of duty" to not mention my old friend Don Rasmussen. Don is Bill's brother and therefore Scott's uncle. Don played a very large and somewhat neglected role in the formation of ESPN. At one point, I believe in the winter of '78–79, Scott and Bill needed to make a down*

payment on the transponder, without which there would be no ESPN. Well as one would expect, at the time, funds were at a premium, as they are with most startups, but this one was more so. Don secured the money for the payment to be made and the transponder to be solidified.

J. B. Doherty

Reams have been written about the Rasmussen credit card legend and ensuing family rows over bucks, so it won't be covered here. See Don Rasmussen's *Just a Guy* if familial flagellation is your gig.

Suffice it to say, their pecuniary input was like a baby's first breath. J. B. Doherty was the obstetrician who slapped baby ESPN's ass so it could squeak and make it out of the delivery room to the nursery.

J. B., at the time, was a young member of the K.S. Sweet investor cadre located in King of Prussia, Pennsylvania. Like much of early ESPN pregnant times, how J. B. came to lead a K.S. Sweet deal which "agreed to fund the operation on a month-to-month basis while working to pull together the business plan and then raise the capital to get on the air" is a Magellan-like tale.

It started in Bill Rasmussen's days with the NHL Hartford Whalers hockey team. Bill lived at Farmington Woods, a golf community experiencing financial woes. J. B. Doherty colleague Tom Cushman was sent to Farmington, representing investors, and met Bill doing a Whalers promotion to boost real estate sales. Later, Bill made an early rescue telephone gasp to Tom Cushman, who invited J. B. to join.

J. B., an engineer and tepid sports fan, was more interested in the satellite technology in Bill and Scott Rasmussen's elevator pitch. Bill spoke of 24-hour sports beamed across America via RCA's Satcom I satellite.

The Doherty family at the time was likely one of a very few that had satellite pedigree. "My dad actually ran a secret base on the California coast from which we put up satellites," he recalled.

At MIT J. B. studied under Dr. Charles Draper, founder of the MIT Instrumentation Laboratory that made the moon landings possible, hence his keen interest in satellites.

While an admitted active but bad athlete, J. B. Doherty was more interested in playing sports than watching them. Yet, his interest in satellites and investor savvy went a long way toward eventually paying off for K.S. Sweet.

So in the part of the deal where K.S. Sweet was to raise the guessti-mated $22 million in capital to get ESPN on the air, again a sports angel seemed to intervene. Both K.S. Sweet and Getty Oil had interests in a Kona Surf Hawaii hotel property, and for various reasons on June 16, 1978, poolside, a bourbon-soaked Getty Oil version of Darth Vader, Stu-art Evey, collided with a Vietnam Marine vet cum investor, J. B. Doherty, and the fuse on the sports big bang was lit.

By then J. B. said he'd pretty much run through his potential partners, and meeting Stu Evey, Getty's man responsible for corporate interests that were not oil related, was the straw that gave ESPN a backbone.

So an MIT engineer, Vietnam vet, satellite-smart angel investor enthuses to Getty's emulation of fictional Hollywood fixer Ray Donovan, aka vice president for diversified operations, and *shazam!* ESPN's in the money.

Lou Palmer

Blood and professional families of Lou ache on baseball's Opening Day, knowing if he was still alive Lou would leap into the season with a passion.

His talent and ability to thrive in the stress of live sports broadcasting was impeccable.

If Lou was Butch Cassidy, I think of myself as his Sundance. We became stronger than friends as we began the ESPN cliffhanger times on exactly the same November 1978 day, as first and second staff members, respectively. Lou covered my darker than white fibs to Bill Rasmussen about my live sports experience.

Lou carried director of programming as an early title. We shared a telephone, splitting our back-to-back joined desks in rented United Cable attic space.

While early Rasmussen suits were sweating the big stuff—investment money and broadcast rights—in the beginning it was up to Lou and I to cobble together a cadre of freelance television teammates to offer samples of our promised wall-to-wall sports telecasts. Many of those freelancers became 'SPNauts.

In prepping this work I connected with Lou's family and learned before he passed he'd composed a manuscript of his own. "Nobody Asked Me" is the title, his daughter Patty told me. For a while she and I tried to get the rest of the family to allow excerpts of Lou's work here. Reading *"Nobody Asked Me"* someday would be a treat. Lou Palmer had a searing way of getting to the point, and his points of view delivered with a twinkle could also buckle knees. I hope his family finds a way to offer it.

I can't help thinking a liquid-induced faux pas I made at his daughter's wedding may have nixed the excerpts. Memory blurs, but during the mandatory "Proud Mary" dance floor melee, I did fall into the bandstand.

Revisiting one of our ESPN postpartum collaborations, Lou and I reminisced:

"You know, ESPN had to work. People watch sports all the time. Those were exciting days, I think about it all the time."

In the Butch and Sundance allegory during our precipice early moments, Sundance would wonder what represented the Joe Lefors institutional character. To Butch it was the suits and money posse.

It reasonably explains Lou's *"Nobody Asked M.e"* Matter of fact, nobody asked us!

Dennis Randall

Years before Dennis Randall and I sat behind a gastrointestinally stricken director in the remote truck of rented television production crews on the evening of ESP's very first telecast, an exhibition UConn basketball game, we'd pass in the city room of the *Hartford Times*.

Dennis was sports editor of the Gannett afternoon paper, succeeding A. B. McGinley, an insurance city icon. I was a sometime State Desk correspondent and full-time national advertising representative.

Walking onto the Grecian-pillared porch of the *Hartford Times*'s stately edifice each work morning, I'd sometimes pause and recall the last election speech of Senator John Kennedy, spoken there hours before he became President-Elect Kennedy.

When I'd see Dennis, it'd be a nod at best. Later Dennis joined the Hartford Whalers hockey franchise and became part of the Whaler exodus to ESPN.

Little did I know as ESPN's founding public relations director that Dennis, Lou Palmer, and I would become joined at the hip producing live satellite-fed sports programs while Bill and Scott Rasmussen traipsed around the country unfolding mirrors to cable television execs while we puffed up smoke in the shape of satellite-delivered sample sports productions.

Lou would be play-by-play, I'd produce, and Dennis would work stats and chyron—jargon for the on-screen caption generator. Giddy and tipsy, during one early event, I asked Dennis to caption "Why Are You Watching?" as we yawned our way through a UConn-hosted triangle gymnastics meet.

We got responses from as far away as Alaska. Later on, Jack Nicklaus told us he bought a satellite dish so he could feed his insatiable appetite for viewing sports of any kind. Our menu of lacrosse, soccer, basketball, baseball, track and field, arm wrestling, log rolling, Aussie football, caber tossing, and golf likely assuaged Jack's appetite.

Dennis Randall's strained professional discipline is epitomized in early ESPN press releases, the subjects of which testify to smoke-and-mirrors elements of the dream, press releases about our headquarters, and a fleet of rolling remote studios that were just the beginning of a PR onslaught we generated from a pair of rented IBM Selectrics.

Jim Stewart

While Dennis Randall, Lou Palmer, and I represented the shaky production tripod that held up the earliest satellite-fed television demonstrations of ESPN's future, we could not have pulled off what still resonates as impossible without the vision and faith of freelance teams led by Jim Stewart, a buttoned-down former colleague. Jim's hands-on production and directing expertise was as impeccable as his personal presentation.

During that demo time, it was Jim Stewart who wrangled a cadre of freelancers , many of whom became 'SPNauts. Jim did not, though he continued to be a go-to freelance director of big ESPN events when his role as communications executive at Connecticut General Insurance allowed.

Bob Bray

Bob Bray was general manager at WHNB TV 30, the NBC Hartford market affiliate, before joining the 'SPNauts in expanding offices at 310 Cooke Street, where United Cable rented us working space in vacant offices and their attic.

Bob Bray's earthy voice was so deep and soft that even when he'd whisper the vibes could be felt. In the traveling road shows that became our early efforts, his management skills were a much needed stable influence for the band of ready-fire-aim promoters we early flyers were.

His penchant for developing management systems for our activity evoked eye-rolling exhales every time he inflicted a new piece of paperwork to crimp our styles. On his birthday it begat a present we had a designer create for Bob. It was a form request form.

Bob Ronstrom

Bob Ronstrom came to the launch pad almost as early as Lou Palmer and I. As a money manager for the World Hockey Association, Bob's quiet style masked the entrepreneurial embers that heated his energy.

Tirelessly he protected the expense swashbucklers, even keeping me away from the threat of a visit to the hoosegow. I'd written a big bouncing personal check to get out of New York with some fancy animation that was COD. Somehow Bob beat the check to my bank with the dough.

Vivian Arsego

The sands of time have covered Vivian's footsteps, though the enthusiasm, loyalty, and friendship that she professionally and personally extended remains vivid.

In a pre-fax, pre-cell, pre–search engine world, Vivian caught the juggled balls we bounced in her direction, making sense of schedules, incoming and outgoing messaging, and where we put our glasses.

Jim Dovey

Jim Dovey was the operating manager of United Cable's Plainville, Connecticut, office which hosted the incubating 'SPNauts with an office, then two more, then an attic full of buzzing staff in the summer of 1979 as the Getty money allowed another exodus, this time from NBC Sports as elsewhere described.

Eric Hansen

Eric was United Cable's senior sales executive who saw the promise of inserting local cable advertising messages into the four minutes per hour that were made available to cable systems who carried ESPN-fed programming.

Eric's Cable Ad Sales company suffered from a soured partnership with Robert Chamberlain.

Robert Chamberlain

Chamberlain's arrogant temperament didn't mix well with Stuart Evey, and Chamberlain's inevitable early exit ensued at ESPN. Chamberlain was accustomed to spending freely, as he wielded a large celebrity and marketing budget for a major insurance company before joining early ESPN.

Knowing Bob as I do, it would not surprise me if he didn't leverage his former Cigna buying clout to get the *New York Times* to publish our launch day full-page ad.

Bob Chamberlain and I had a rocky relationship too, details of which spill later.

The Unknown Sony Salesman

One of my favorite stories involves the morning an invited Sony videotape distributor sent a junior sales fellow to our Plainville attic offices. I expect when we had to take him up the stairs and under the rafters to sit with us, he must have gotten cotton mouth seeing our slapstick operation.

So when he asked me how much videotape we wanted to purchase, I watched his eyes go from squint to deer in the headlights as we described our needs.

Remember digital then was finger counting, and videotape was migrating downward from two- to one-inch formats for broadcast quality. I wish I could remember his name to offer attribution to the calculating that we went through as I said, we'd need videotape for 24 hours every day, 365 days a year, forever, and ¾-inch videotape to record highlights of football, basketball, baseball, hockey, and other sports for our multiple *SportsCenter* programs every day and night.

Four decades later as digital disrupted film and video, and on the cusp of the artificial intelligence explosion, it's sobering to remember shooting sports news on 16-millimeter positive film that was edited by stapling highlights together.

Those thoughts trigger wondering about quantum computing and how it will bring more sports reality into the homes of high-rolling sports gamblers willing to invest in the latest betting edge that technology can offer . . . sort of like the edge the open *SportsCenter* phone lines into pro football locker rooms gave us in 1979.

MONEY MANNA
Sid Petersen

Sidney Petersen became chairman and CEO of Getty Oil shortly after I met him and before I came to befriend his son Chris, who joined ESPN as a certified 'SPNaut.

As Getty president Mr. Petersen hosted a meeting for the few of us who visited the Getty headquarters and was responsible for the top-level approval.

Later, Chairman Petersen would not be pleased when his son Chris took a job with ESPN via other connections he had developed elsewhere. Chris put his college in mothballs while he joined the sports television revolution.

Chris's dad had this answer to his grandson Tyler's questions, in an interview during Tyler's University of Oregon work toward a journalism and communications degree.

Q: How did Getty Oil help create ESPN?

A: At that time (1978) Getty Oil was flush with cash; we had more cash than we were able to successfully invest back into the oil business. We didn't want to just go out and drill a dry hole, so we started looking around for other things. One of the things we did, we spent about $600 million to buy an insurance company. And later we came across this venture capital project, by Bill (Rasmussen). He had this idea about setting up an all-sports television network.

He said if you invest $15 million, in a short period, three to five years, you will have built a business that you can sell for $25 or $30 million. We bought into that concept, thinking for us, $15 million was a drop in the bucket and the returns looked good. Well in three years, the company had accomplished the plan that we had laid out.

And then they came back and said, if you invest $25 million more, then in three to five years, it will be worth $100 million! And so we did that, and sure enough in five years, it was. About that time, Getty was acquired by Texaco, and Texaco was not interested in being in the cable TV business so they dumped it to ABC, who subsequently was acquired by Disney. Getty was acquired by Texaco in 1984, and by 1986, ESPN was already making more money than ABC was. It (ESPN) has really been successful.

Q: So Getty got into the cable business strictly for its potential profitability?

A: Yes, we never intended to be long-term broadcasters. It was strictly a venture capital opportunity. If we had owned ESPN for a little longer, I am sure we would have looked to sell it to a company like ABC as Texaco did. The board of directors, quite honestly, was never happy with us being in the broadcast business.

Because from that little peanut operation, whatever we invested $10 million here, $25 million there, they got TWICE as much news press as the oil company did.

The media is interested in itself, the media. ESPN was getting all kinds of write-ups and news in other media outlets, and our directors were not comfortable with that. We never emphasized to them what was going on, except the returns (laughs).

I could have killed that whole thing (funding ESPN) but I liked the idea.

From what I learned, Sid Petersen might very well have killed ESPN if his business judgement had not prevailed.

Stuart Evey

Without Stuart Evey, bullish and brilliant, in this work bearing my anointment as Darth Vader, ESPN would not exist, had his ego and Getty Oil leverage not put up the money to birth our daydreams.

Evey said, "J. Paul Getty, the richest man in the world had depended on me to produce solutions, no matter what the conditions."

Given Evey's Hollywood peccadillos he brings to mind a mid-20th-century version of the fictional Ray Donovan.

Evey's politically polite perch in the Getty hierarchy as its vice president of diversified operations was supported by George Conner, finance manager of Evey's world. Conner agrees if it weren't for Evey and his Hollywood ways, there was no way the ESPN money deal would have happened.

The Evey/Conner-supervised $55 million eventual ESPN investment was five-and-a-half times the fingers-crossed early estimates, but nary a ripple in the nearly $9 billion of other Getty Oil estimated worth in that era.

Sharing affinity and afflictions Stuart Evey and I were high-functioning drunks. When we met he was surely at economic strata clouds above mine, but nonetheless we were both nurtured as street urchins, who mutually developed playing all sorts of angles in tobacco-filled poolrooms of our youths.

It was destined that we do combat, the first round being a booze bout on his turf, Hollywood's famous Brown Derby during the ESPN money courtship.

The knockout punch came on the evening of ESPN's launch when he brought into the studio an Evey-designed directors' chair with his name and "executive producer"—the title Bill Rasmussen had given me—emblazoned across its back support.

That incident spun me, along with a Smirnoff-soaked ego, off the precarious ledge a modicum of talent had kept me from falling over, lasting longer than many of the earliest 'SPNauts who were purged in the housecleaning Getty money and Evey control leveraged.

The space occupied by the ensuing paragraphs should appear at the happy ending section of a saga, but in varying form, Stu Evey and I surrendered to booze.

Again, in his words, post-ESPN: "I was emotionally bankrupt: I needed to do something. I had known for some time that alcohol had the huge potential to get me into a lot of trouble. Some instances that combined my imposing ego with demon alcohol were just too close for comfort."

Stuart Evey wrote those words in his 2004 *Creating an Empire*, in which he told of his sobering journey to and at the Betty Ford Institute, 19 years earlier.

Me? After flunking rehab in 1982, it finally took hold in 1987. In 1989 I returned to ESPN for a season in order to leave on good terms.

Stu and I are due for a good sarsaparilla bout, somewhere soon.

George Conner

When Stu Evey sent George Conner to oversee the Getty investment in ESPN, little did George know he'd replace a sumptuous office in the Getty building that sported an executive bar and lounge with a tiny shared office where he was scrunched in with 'SPNaut and accountant Bob Ronstrom.

Post-ESPN, George spent a beach break at Marina Del Rey that turned into five years of day trading. He had decided to leave Getty Oil after ESPN "because nothing could be as exciting as what we did. I just wouldn't trade those three and a half years at ESPN for anything in the world."

Deftly calling his boss Stu Evey controversial and able to "really alienate a lot of people," George recounted how Evey would call him before he'd have to approve millions more in the escalating Getty invest-ments and ask if he should.

"I never wavered a millisecond that it was going to do well. It was just the enthusiasm of everybody that was there, and I just had a gut feeling, so Stu would just get us millions more," George says.

George Conner's early ESPN recollections are so vivid and so important was his 'SPNaut role that when we asked if he'd contribute to this book his answer required a full chapter of its own (chapter 3).

THE NBC CAVALRY
In the honest bones of the ESPN insemination team lurked a valid inse-curity that the prospect of building a worldwide leader in sports televi-sion might just be a tad above our pay grades.

At least it lurked in these bones. Stu Evey saw it, and once the Getty gusher began to flow he shanghaied a pair of big-name sports execu-tives from NBC. They brought along with them a cadre of experienced network support talent, necessary yet often patronizing to the earliest 'SPNauts.

After a fast period of molting, the sides blended and got on with the work of revolutionizing sports.

Chet Simmons
If ever there was a precursor to ESPN, it was *ABC's Wide World of Sports*. Who could forget Vinko Bogataj's ski-jumping agony of defeat?

Chet Simmons joined Edgar Sherick's Sports Programs, Inc. *Wide World's* creator, where another TV sports legend, Roone Arledge also flourished as ABC bought them, turning 1960s Saturday-afternoon tele-vision into an anthology of offbeat and on-beat sports.

Simmons went on to become president of NBC Sports, and in a timely move to ESPN in 1979 during the peacock network's whis-pered sports power struggle with Don Ohlmeyer, Simmons not only took NBC's manager of sports programs, Scotty Connal, with him, but announcer Jim Simpson and a cadre of middle management and junior producers.

The Entertainment and Sports Programming Network Inc.

319 COOKE STREET □ PLAINVILLE, CONNECTICUT 06062 □ 203-747-6847

NBC's Simmons
New ESPN President

FOR IMMEDIATE RELEASE, JULY 18, 1979

PLAINVILLE, Conn.—The Entertainment and Sports Programming Network has named Chester R. Simmons, a pioneer in the field of television sports, as President and Chief Operating Officer of the cable network that will begin full-time sports programming, via satellite, in September of this year.

The announcement was made today by William F. Rasmussen, Chairman of the Board and Chief Executive Officer of ESPN.

Simmons comes to ESPN from the National Broadcasting Company (NBC) where he has been President of the Sports Division since November of 1977. In his 15 years with NBC, Simmons has also served as Vice-President of Sports, Vice-President of Sports Operations and Director of Sports. He joined the network in 1964.

Born in Manhattan and raised in Ossining, N.Y., and Pawtucket, R.I., Simmons began his television career with Sports Programs, Inc., an independent production company that worked with and eventually evolved into the American Broadcasting Company (ABC) Sports Department. He was Vice-President and General Manager of ABC Sports during that time.

"The ESPN concept of television sports 24 hours a day is an exciting challenge for me," said Simmons. "I was there during the inception of ABC Sports and the rebirth of NBC Sports and I see many similarities between those beginnings and the beginning of ESPN.

"There's no question that cable television sports is at the same stage right now that network sports was 15 or 20 years ago. It's a thing of the future. I've lived through the evolution of sports on television and what lies ahead for cable TV is incalculable at this point."

While with ABC, Simmons was deeply involved in the original television package with the American Football League (now the American Football Conference of the National Football League) and has worked closely with the AFC telecasts now being shown on NBC.

He was instrumental in starting "Wide World of Sports" for ABC and 18 years later, became involved in the birth and growth of NBC's "Sportsworld." Simmons also brought pro hockey and college basketball to NBC and was one of the people who led the network's effort that secured the 1980 Summer Olympics.

"Chet Simmons is one of the most highly-respected men in sports television and we are very fortunate that he has agreed to join ESPN," said Rasmussen. "He will be in charge of one of the most mammoth production challenges ever undertaken.

"Chet's knowledge of all areas of TV sports will be invaluable and his experience in helping start the sports department at ABC and in the evolution of NBC Sports will greatly benefit ESPN as we prepare to launch our all-sports network for cable television."

Simmons has a Bachelor of Arts degree in broadcasting from the University of Alabama and did his graduate work at Boston University. He served in the U.S. Coast Guard from 1951 to 1954 and presently resides in Old Greenwich, Conn., with his wife, Harriet, and four children.

"The progress that ESPN has made in a short period of time is fantastic," said Simmons. "There's no question that ESPN's arrangement with the NCAA (National Collegiate Athletic Association) is a major breakthrough and the public becomes the recipient of the outstanding sports competition that the NCAA has to offer.

"Cable TV can go into areas and depth that network television cannot offer. We have all the time in the world so we are not restricted the same way the networks are."

In point of time, Simmons is the senior person in network sports broadcasting right now.

-30-

CONTACT: DENNIS RANDALL/MIKE CARUSO (203) 747-6847

Chet Simmons press release

COURTESY DENNIS RANDALL

Simmons and Connal were the cavalry ESPN needed. Their Rolodexes alone added millions in value. They recruited NCOs Barry Black, Jim Dullaghan, Joe Gianquinto, Todd Matheus, Jim Huey, and Ellen Beckwith.

One memorable moment, the weekend we launched, was when *SportsCenter* asked Chet if we had the rights to use NBC, ABC, and CBS sports highlights on our air.

"Just use them. I'll straighten it out. They all owe me," Simmons said.

Chet Simmons could be incendiary. Connal had a calming effect. Both put their kids to work at ESPN.

Jed Simmons, now a major voice on innovation and invention in academia and industry, remembers those days when he saw his dad more than the rest of the family because he took a 1979 summer internship at ESPN before winging off to college and a big business career.

Scotty Connal

To the hundreds of young lives that Scotty Connal touched, his greatest accomplishment is their loyalty and dedication. The ESPN peach fuzz gang continue to admire Connal, with most speaking to his leadership qualities.

Many don't realize the amazing history-laden stories that bear Scotty Connal's name. On Sunday, November 24, 1963, he decided to live telecast the transfer of Lee Harvey Oswald from the Dallas Police to the County Jail, which became the only live footage of Jack Ruby murdering Oswald.

On November 17, 1968—ten years prior to ESPN's first-ever telecast, a UConn exhibition basketball game—Connal's career reached a low point as he and Simmons were frustratingly involved in one of televised sports greatest flubs, the notorious Heidi game in which they gave way to pressure from network suits to air the movie *Heidi* at a hard 7:00 p.m. Eastern Time instead of the game's exciting finish.

The Jets-Raiders game—forever named the Heidi Bowl—was preempted turned out to be one of the greatest comebacks in the history of the NFL. Oakland scored twice in the last minute to win 42–32.

ESPnews

The Entertainment and Sports Programming Network Inc.

319 COOKE STREET ☐ PLAINVILLE, CONNECTICUT 06062 ☐ 203-747-6847

ESPN Names Connal
Senior Vice-President

FOR IMMEDIATE RELEASE, AUGUST 7, 1979:

PLAINVILLE, CT---Allan B. (Scotty) Connal, a man with a wealth of television experience from 32 years at the National Broadcasting Company (NBC), has been named Senior Vice-President of Operations and Production for the Entertainment and Sports Programming Network of Plainville, Conn.

Chester R. Simmons, President of ESPN, made the announcement today. ESPN will begin full-time sports programming, via RCA's Satcom I, Transponder #7, to cable television systems across the country at 7 p.m. (EDT) on Sept. 7, 1979.

Connal, Vice-President, Sports Operations for NBC since February of 1978, will be in charge of program operations, technical operations and production for ESPN. He is recognized as a leader in sports production and the man responsible for many innovations in television sports coverage.

"No one in sports broadcasting has the experience and expertise in the areas of production, programming and operations as Scotty Connal," said Simmons. "He is the perfect person to take on the biggest television sports challenge anywhere.

"With ESPN, he will be able to build a staff from the ground up. His presence will attract some of the most highly-experienced people from around the country."

Connal, who attended Columbia University and the University of Heidelberg (Germany), began with NBC in the Guest Relations Department in 1947. He worked in all phases of the NBC operation, but zeroed in on sports 15 years ago and worked as Administrator of Sports, Manager of Sports Programs, Executive Producer and Vice-President, Sports Operations.

As Executive Producer, Connal won an Emmy for his coverage of the memorable 1975 World Series between Boston and Cincinnati which featured one of the greatest sports shots of all time--- Carlton Fisk's reaction to his game-winning home run in the sixth game that gave the Red Sox a series-tying 7-6 victory in the bottom of the 12th inning.

Connal is considered the father and developer of TV isolation. Under his direction, NBC has become the top network in sports production and Connal's expertise has been put to good use in such major events as the Super Bowl, Rose and Orange Bowls, the 1972 Winter Olympics in Japan, the national basketball championships, college and professional football and many major golf tournaments.

Prior to moving into the sports area, Connal was a unit manager for news, assigned to such projects as national political conventions, presidential elections and United States space shots.

"The ESPN concept represents a tremendous challenge for me," said Connal. "It is very stimulating and has come along at the right time in my career. It's something that's never been done (full-time sports programming) and that makes it very exciting.

"I have worked with Chet Simmons for 15 years at NBC and I feel that we can make ESPN No. 1 in sports television just as we made NBC No. 1. Chet and Bill Rasmussen (ESPN Chairman of the Board) are top professionals and it will be a pleasure working with both of them."

Connal became Administrator of Sports for NBC in 1964, was Manager, Sports Programs from 1965 to 1972, Executive Producer from 1972 to 1978 and Vice-President, Sports Operations since February of 1978.

A New York native, Connal and his wife, Mathilda, have eight children and reside in Old Greenwich, Conn.

-30-

CONTACT: DENNIS RANDALL/MIKE CARUSO (203) 747-6847

Scotty Connal press release

COURTESY DENNIS RANDALL

Later, Scotty indelibly ingrained the image of Red Sox Carlton Fisk's emphatic body English waving of a home-run ball in Game 6 of the 1975 World Series. The image flew in the face of TV dictum to follow the ball. Connal commanded, "Stay on Fisk," and the iconic gem was created.

Equally iconic is the Scotty Connal protégé Chris Berman, who recalls Connal coaching that eschewed teleprompters, saying Scotty said "I want you talking to the lens, or looking at your co-anchor and just be talking sports with them or the viewer." Later Berman tells how Connal hired him years before ESPN started.

At ESPN his Connal calm was legend, especially in assuaging Simmons's equally legendary ire. His family, Bruce, Linda, and Cathy, followed their dad into the sports television world.

One of Scotty's hires, Bill Shanahan, describes Scotty Connal's instinctive interviewing this way:

I arrived at the United Cable TV building on a hot, humid August afternoon, and was directed up the stairs to ESPN. The door was open, and just behind it, sort of blocking easy, unhindered access was a folding table, covered with loose piles of paper. Seated behind the table was a tallish, lean figure, balding, and with glasses pushed up and perched on his forehead.

The space behind him was basically a large, unfinished attic, with the building's roof structure visible and lined with insulation. There were other folding tables with telephones, ashtrays, paper piles, many cardboard boxes with more papers, and people talking in small groups or on the phone or staring at the many papers.

I stood in the doorway, taking in my first glimpse of the Entertainment and Sports Programming Network, and the man at the table looked up and said, "Can I help you?" I said I was here to see Mr. Connal. He replied, "I'm Scotty Connal."

While still standing in the doorway, my interview was quick and a bit brusque. Scotty, glasses now down on his nose, was only mildly interested in my production experience, and quickly moved on to compensation . . . and near disaster.

When he asked what I was currently paid at my Washington job, he started shaking his head and said that it wouldn't work because the associate producer position pay was 25 percent less, and he didn't want to hire anyone who had to take a pay cut because they might become resentful. Space and time again stopped for a moment as I felt opportunity start to evaporate.

I remember literally raising my right hand as in a courtroom and saying something like, "Mr. Connal, I swear that whatever happens down the road with this job, I'll never make the starting pay an issue."

There was a long pause. The glasses went back up to the forehead, a hand went up to rub his eyes, and he said, "OK, go talk to that guy over there." Forty-four years later I still remember the feeling of having dodged one of the biggest bullets in my life.

I thanked Mr. Connal and started in the direction he indicated, when, from behind, I heard his voice, "Wait a minute!" I turned around.

He said to me, "You're not a sonofabitch, are you?"

I think my first response to this novel job interview question was "Umm. . . ." Fortunately I followed with something like, "No, I don't think so."

He replied, "OK. I've worked with a lot of sonofabitches and I don't want any here."

In a single, almost surreal experience lasting maybe five minutes, I was introduced not only to Scotty Connal's character but to what was to be the character of this attic-dwelling TV network.

Personally, I always felt that a close relationship with John Barleycorn kept me from enjoying the full acceptance of Scotty Connal. An avid athlete and competitor, he coached and pitched the ESPN softball team with the same vigor and demanding attendance that he did in our studio.

Relegated to Scotty's softball bench for most of the team's original game, he begrudgingly inserted me into softball's geek field—right field in layman's terms.

As it turned out, in a game-saving moment my body somehow remembered the athlete it used to be and snared a line drive in an over-the-shoulder catch that ended the inning in a tied game.

We went on to win the game and later Scotty's eyes met mine, and a moment of respect ensued that I still savor. Then we went on to business as usual.

Joe Gianquinto, Jim Huey, Barry Black, Jim Dullaghan, Ellen Beckwith, and Pam Jones made up most of the Simmons and Connal New York posse that got a culture shock when they got to the ESPN

1980 ESPN softball team, family, and fans. Players, L–R, front row: Bob Scanlon, Frank Casarella, Scotty Connal; middle row, L–R: Dave Ogrean, Ellen Beckwith; back row, L–R: Jim Huey, Todd Matheus.
PHOTO COURTESY ELLEN BECKWITH

headquarters in the attic of United Cable while the new network's studio and headquarters was being built.

After treatment their latent opportunity vision kicked in and they hopped aboard the chaotic train that took a posse of all-sports television believers to a dreamland, only to wake up months later to find out it was not a dream, nor a nightmare.

STICKS AND MORTAR
Geoff Bray
Geoff Bray, like many of us, was young, ready, willing and excited. Geoff's 'SPNaut proven pedigree lies in his professional capacity as ESPN's founding architect.

So often the term "architect" is casually attached to people who start things. Not Geoff Bray.

Geoff is the pro architect who designed and attended to the bricks and mortar construction of our threshold building, now rumored to be a teardown target, though downsizing for economy's sake at ESPN may rescue our original home.

Geoff Bray's architectural chops were great. His television chops were not, so together he and I visited the then state-of-the-art Broadcast House which housed WFSB Channel 3, where I'd just left as promotion producer. Geoff's eyes widened considerably as he absorbed the needs of a full-blown TV facility.

At the time of our visit, the exodus to ESPN by key employees there had not begun, so we were welcomed and given the grand tour. Bob Bray, formerly general manager at WHNB Channel 30, arranged for another perspective, WHNB being a less financially endowed production facility.

Geoff's initial pencil designs were also supported by the scribbles of Bill and Scott Rasmussen, who excitedly drew their thoughts in a caffeine-fueled late night, turning over their legal-pad imaginations to Geoff.

And then to my surprise Geoff produced handwritten notes which were from me, Lou Palmer, and Bill Rasmussen offering our thoughts regarding his original plans. To my everlasting red face and in recovery jargon, a well-treasured green thought, is my attempt at humor and tell-tale 11th comment asking the intended whereabouts of the bar.

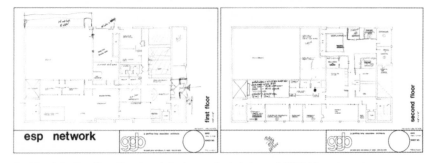

Architect G. Geoffrey Bray's original pencil sketches of ESPN headquarters
COURTESY G. GEOFFREY BRAY

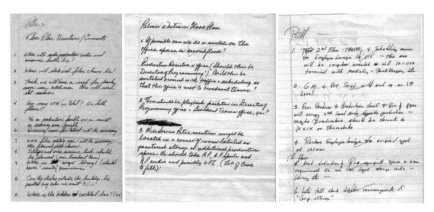

Handwritten comments to Geoffrey Bray re: original architectural plans, from (L–R) Peter Fox, Lou Palmer, and Bill Rasmussen
COURTESY G. GEOFFREY BRAY

Researching this work, Geoff and I planned on touring our rooms of remembering, and after a pair of attempts were told by communications gatekeepers the network was too busy to accommodate a tour by its founding architect and executive producer.

Like kids with their noses squished against a pane, we lunched nearby and shot a wistful picture of Geoff from the directly across-the-street driveway of the 916–924 Middle Street Apartments, site of many Bolivian marching powder fueled off-the-clock 'SPNaut rages.

BUSINESS BUILDING

Earliest network business building began once more with a Whalers hockey team influence as Scott Rasmussen's onetime roommate and workmate there donned the 'SPNaut uniform and became a leader in convincing the cable television world to join the sports revolution.

Jim Bates

Jim Bates on the business side of ESPN was a true 'SPNaut who parlayed his intimate knowledge of early cable sports programming into a remarkable career that included similar bootstrapping with the infant

Golf Channel and as general manager of SportsChannel New York, among others.

But, most of all Jim Bates was probably the earliest of ESPN marketing types who knew in his belly the ride we were about to take in 1978, because he was Scott Rasmussen's good friend, roommate, and hockey teammate.

Here are Jim's thoughts on the earliest days of ESPN:

"I Was There at the Beginning." . . . "No You Weren't"

Invariably, over the years, that conversation took place several times, when I'd meet someone who claimed they were at ESPN in the "beginning." I'd always ask, "well, where did you work?" The reply was always the same, "Bristol." My reply, met with a blank stare was, "Well, you weren't there at the beginning because if you were you would've said 319 Cooke Street." That is where ESPN began.

My journey to ESPN and what ultimately became a dynamic industry, cable, had a rather circuitous route. It began, in the summer of 1975 when my summer job was working for the New England Whalers of the then World Hockey Association. Today, they are the Carolina Hurricanes of the National Hockey League. I began as the receptionist, stuffing envelopes and answering the phone. I did it all however in my five years there—you name it I did it. It was a truly special experience, especially for a college kid, and it ultimately led me to the cable industry.

During my five-year stint as a part-time employee with the Whalers, while attending college, I got to know and work with Bill and Scott Rasmussen, ESPN's cofounders. Bill came into the office on a daily basis, so I knew him, but I saw Scott a bit more sporadically during that first summer. However, the Whalers I found out had a "front office" hockey team, during the winter, and upon arriving for the first game I found out that Scott was the goalie. That was the beginning of a friendship that lasts to this day.

At some point, Scott got a condo at 2 Maple Lane in Avon, CT. Since my parents lived down in New Haven at the time, I lived with Scott during the summer of '77 and then later on, when ESPN began. Anyway, we had some fun that summer of '77, doing what college kids did before the iPhone, social media, and cable TV.

In the summer of '78, Scott and I were driving in the car when he told me that he and his dad were developing a business for cable TV and they'd like me to be a part of it. My first response was "cool," followed closely by, "what's cable TV?" I had no idea, but I would come to find out I was not alone and cable was somewhat embryonic in those days.

Throughout the time period of '78 until the spring of '79, I would be receiving updates from Scott on the progress of the developing ESP network. (Note: I won't go into the original concept as I'm sure that'll be covered elsewhere.) I do believe, to this day, that I was in the first 10 people to know of the existence of what became ESPN. I do know, I became the 14th full-time employee.

As things continued I'd see Scott at Whaler games, where he was the announcer and I the press box and press room attendant. We also played on some hockey teams together so our encounters were frequent and varied, along with a few stops at the various "watering holes." By the spring of 1979, things were coming together and it looked as though Getty Oil would be the principal funder of the operation.

In late May I began on a part-time basis and then full-time on or around June 6th, reporting to 319 Cooke Street. At the same time, Scott hired another "friend," Jeff James, and the two of us would be "affiliate representatives." Neither of us knew a thing about cable TV, so enter Ron Newman. Ron was the recently hired vice president of affiliate relations, and his job was to oversee the distribution of ESPN to the various cable operators around the country. Jeff and I would be doing the same, but on a smaller scale. (Note: Cable at the time was in about 20 million homes, mostly rural.)

I remember vividly Ron being a little exasperated about our lack of knowledge, but at the same time, taught us the industry. He had come from Madison Square Garden in NY so had a good cable background before many people even had heard of it. He did a wonderful job and I remember the setting, the lessons, and his patience still to this day.

In those days, the systems were generally small "Mom and Pop" operations, where the big decision was whether they would buy "one of those earth station things." Without it they couldn't get ESPN, so it was an important piece to our overall success. My first phone call was to a fellow in Arkansas, H .E. McCullough. He wasn't there, he was "out on the pole." Which pole, I have no idea, just the pole. OK I say, I'll call back. Jeff and I worked both ends of the Cable Fact Book, a telephone-type book listing every cable system by state.

We were a small band of people operating out of the then United Cable office at 319 Cooke Street in Plainville, CT. The cable system had the lower floor and we had the second half of the lower floor and then began expanding upstairs, which we completely took over. Then we expanded further and went into the attic, when the NBC folks arrived. It was quite something seeing these big NY executives working out of an attic.

I believe it safe to say, we all knew we were a part of something neat but we had no idea how neat. The general population thought we were nuts . . . 24 hours a day of sports was a ridiculous idea. No one knew what it was and when you told them you received a blank stare in return.

I remember the first convention Jeff and I went to. It was the CATA convention held at Lake Geneva, Wisconsin, in July of 1979. Our office colleague, Carol La Cart, got married on that Saturday and afterward Jeff and I departed for Milwaukee and a short drive to Lake Geneva. We arrived, fairly late in the evening, and entered a condo that was occupied . . . interesting, it was, as we heard noises coming from the upstairs. Anyway, back we go and get a new condo and head off to sleep, having very little idea of what the next day would bring. It would be the first of the many conventions I'd attend over my 35-plus years in the cable industry.

As we moved into July, Chet Simmons arrived and he brought with him a cadre of NBC folks from New York. This was the decision of Getty, who had become the principal owner of ESP and it probably was the right decision. For the uninitiated, like me, it was a lesson of "he who controls the checkbook has the power." Getty had and controlled the checkbook.

Ron Newman

Ron Newman was hired as vice president of affiliate relations, and his job was to oversee the distribution of ESPN to the various cable operators around the country. He came from the MSG (Madison Square Garden) network—one of the few other operating satellite-fed cable networks.

Ron's tenure at ESPN fell victim to the Getty-funded and Evey-directed takeover of the network, devastating him, according to his wife Wendy, who offered these remarks in her late husband's stead.

Ron's adventure with ESPN started in the early part of 1979. We were living in New Jersey and Ron was working for Madison Square Garden Sports as their marketing manager.

The Entertainment and Sports Programming Network Inc.
319 COOKE STREET □ PLAINVILLE, CONNECTICUT 06062 □ 203-747-6847

NEWMAN NAMED
ESPN VICE-PRESIDENT

FOR IMMEDIATE RELEASE

PLAINVILLE, Conn. — Ron Newman, 34, Marketing Manager for Madison Square Garden Sports since last May, has been named Vice-President of the Entertainment and Sports Programming Network, it has been announced by ESPN President William F. Rasmussen.

Raised in Haverstraw, N.Y., and Mt. Olive Township, N.J., Newman will be in charge of affiliate relations for ESPN, which means he will have full responsibility for sales and servicing of the network's affiliates across the country. He performed similar duties for Madison Square Garden Sports.

"We are fortunate to have secured the services of a man of Ron Newman's stature," said Rasmussen. "He has been a leader in sales marketing throughout his career and his knowledge of the cable television industry will be very valuable to ESPN."

Newman is a graduate of the State University of New York at New Paltz (1966) and began his career in cable television as sales director for Rockland Cable Vision of Rockland County, N.Y., in 1971 after working in college administration at City University of New York and Fitch College of New York.

"The position with ESPN is the best opportunity of my life," said Newman. "ESPN has the potential to become the biggest sports programming service in the country and I'm excited to be part of it. I am looking forward to the challenge of my new job."

Newman will begin his duties with ESPN in the near future.

-30-

CONTACT: DENNIS RANDALL (203)747-6847

Ron Newman press release
COURTESY DENNIS RANDALL

While attending cable shows and conventions he met Bill Rasmussen and Bill talked about the idea of ESPN. Ron was intrigued and thought the opportunity was something special.

He even talked to Ted Turner who told Ron to "go for it." Ron had a very close relationship with Turner via his WTBS and pending CNN cable news leader.

In March of 1979 Bill offered Ron the position as VP, marketing. Ron loved a good title. In April Ron moved to Connecticut, staying at the Farmington Motor Inn. On weekends I would either drive or fly up to go house hunting because Ron thought this would be it. I had a great career doing marketing research for Parke Davis/Warner Lambert and was less than thrilled about the move, but I wanted to be supportive and have him follow his dream.

We found a condo and moved in in July 1979. I remember Ron working tirelessly with the small staff on Cooke Street in Plainville. It was a trying time. I recall meeting George Conner. I had a bad feeling about him.

In September there was buzz that NBC was going to take over and bring their own people in. By the time of the launch it was pretty well known that it was going to happen.

When Ron was let go in November he was devastated. At that point he vowed never to work for anyone ever again and he didn't, creating his own marketing company.

Evan Baker

Evan Baker led a marketing team that by Groundhog Day after the launch was able to offer this report:

In the four months since ESPN first began broadcasting our total programming hours have exceeded 2,000. This represents more total sports hours than ABC, NBC and CBS carry on a combined basis for an entire year.

ESPN is currently averaging fourteen hours of programming per day and it is planned that during the first quarter of 1980 or shortly thereafter we expect to reach 24 hours of continuous programming each day.

It is anticipated that by the end of the first quarter of 1980 ESPN will reach 4 million households and by the end of the year, the projection is increased to 6 million households.

ESPN has established a New York sales office headed by Michael Presbrey as Vice President, Advertising Sales. Other members of the staff include Bob Jeremiah, and Annette Leiderman, account executives and Patti Nolan, Director of Client Relations.

ESPN's current list of clients include Anheuser-Busch, Wall Street Journal, *Barron's, Smithsonian, Pontiac, English Leather, Mazda, Magnavox, Noxzema, and Mobil Oil.*

FACES AND VOICES

From the voice of **Lee Leonard** came the words first cast into space to eventually reverberate in historical recountings of ESPN's birthday. I dare not violate the axiom: "If you love sports . . . if you really love sports, you'll think you've died and gone to sports heaven."

Next to Leonard on the original *SportsCenter* set, built by my many-time vendor, Harold Post, sat **George Grande,** sporting a cherubic young face that hid an encyclopedia of sports minutia.

Now George hides a collection of ESPN stories he told me he promised to only reveal when Chet Simmons, Scotty Connal, Bill Rasmussen, and George Conner write their books.

I know Bill is done, having written a pair, and Chet and Scotty didn't get to theirs, while George Conner has provided a pretty comprehensive memory here.

I hope someday I can read George Grande's recollections, which I know would be as eloquent as his on-air presence.

SportsCenter Madhouse: Left side front to back: Lou Palmer, Fred Muzzy, Bill Shanahan, and perhaps Ellen Beckwith. Right side front to back: George Grande, Lee Leonard.
COURTESY BILL RASMUSSEN

Bob Waller, Bob Ley, Tom Mees, Chris Berman, and **Lou Palmer** filled out the early on-camera cadre, joining Leonard and Grande in a *SportsCenter* production madhouse that made cat herding look like a spectator sport.

TECH TEAM
Ralph Voight

ESPN's founding chief engineer Ralph Voight is ever burned into the memory of this chronicler. In the tradition of the "plastics, Benjamin, plastics" advisory to Dustin Hoffman's Benjamin Braddock in *The Graduate*, Ralph on our analog-driven launch night cornered me and advised:

"Remember I said this Peter, digital . . . digital."

An otherwise stoic personality, his talent and management in those hectic moments were reassuring and continued to be until he retired almost 10 years later to continue dabbling in the radio amateur world where Ralph was known by his call sign, N2OK.

Steve Myers

Steve Myers was a good friend of Ralph Voight and succumbed to Ralph's recruiting. His decision to join ESPN may very well have been affected by the earlier exodus of several of the technical staff he supervised at Hartford's WFSB.

He's revered by the team he built for Ralph at ESPN. "I was very impressed on how the staff loved and admired Steve Myers," said a then-recent hire, adding: "We all referred to Steve as Steve, unless he was showing someone around the place, then he was referred to as Mr. Myers."

Chuck Pagano et al.

A true 'SPNaut is Chuck, Steve Myers's backup and later a Sports Broadcasting Hall of Famer and winner of multiple Emmy awards for technological wizardry. Chuck Pagano's bearish common-man style endeared him to engineering peers and suits.

Another Hartford WFSB escapee, Chuck followed **Tony Valentino** from the CBS affiliate and lured **Bill Lamb** from WTNH New Haven to

Seven ways to be an agency hero.

 Thurs. Fri. Sat. Sun.

Be shrewd, reach 18-34 year old men on the new ESPN Total-Sports Network.

1st Way: ESPN starts its round-the-clock, nationwide telecasts tonight, September 7th. That means that from here on in you can offer a sports-starved client a franchise position on top-quality major sports programming at low cost. The kind of franchise other advertisers spend megabucks for. Including over 50 NCAA major football games and nearly 200 key NCAA basketball games, plus top-notch professional golf and tennis. We'll be offering that kind of programming every day of the week.

2nd Way: You'll be offering him tremendous efficiency against the young, upscale market, including those elusive 18-34's. And we guarantee 4.5 million high-income cable households right from the start. (Ask us for the new Nielsen demographic research data now available.)

3rd Way: You can give him real frequency. He can reach those young males several times a day, every day.

4th Way: You can offer him sponsorship. We're offering 1/8 and 1/16 sponsorships of major NCAA events. Scatter plans are also available.

5th Way: You can promise your client an absence of clutter. There'll be an average of only 5 minutes of commercial announcements per hour.

6th Way: You'll give him a chance to be an innovative leader in the explosive trend to cable—by '81, over thirty percent of all TV homes will be receiving cable.

7th Way: You'll be offering him a vehicle that's a proven success, already purchased by Anheuser-Busch and other alert advertisers.

ESPN, the Entertainment and Sports Programming Network, a subsidiary of Getty Oil, offers you action-oriented programming, a unique opportunity to get the male audience most network television isn't delivering. To learn more about what we can do for you and your client, call Bob Chamberlain at 203-584-8477. You can bet we'll be hearing from your opposite number in the other agency.

If you've got the spots, we've got the sports.

ESPN
THE TOTAL SPORTS
CABLE NETWORK

Chuck Pagano, Broadcasting Hall of Famer

form the triad of live control-room switchers, a skill requiring the focus and nerve you might find in high-stakes poker.

Russel Gabay rode the audio while Tony ran the Grass Valley switcher from the parked WHYY remote truck serving as the launch control room, because our control room was still under construction at the time of Bill's launch promise to the cable industry. Chuck relieved Tony.

Pagano laughs that he cut his commute in half by joining ESPN, but adds he also pretty much doubled his salary when chief engineer Ralph Voight recruited him, once again raiding the local affiliate of top-shelf talent.

Between Pagano, Lamb, and Valentino the trio kept ESPN control-room switching duties going while the complex was being built around itself, the control room being the WHYY remote truck parked alongside the in-progress construction.

Exhausted, the trio added **Mitch Rymanowski** to the key control-switching quartet as the round-the-clock sports programming kicked in.

Chuck, Mitch, and Tony were among the WFSB Hartford tech exodus that included **Jerry Weed, Bob Schlenker, Ralph Eno,** and **Jeff Israel**.

As Chuck Pagano served his notice at WFSB to his boss **Steve Myers**, Pagano says Myers's response was "Oh, God, the shit's going to hit the fan on this one," meaning Myers's big boss.

And not many weeks later Myers, succumbing to his longtime close friend Ralph Voight's recruiting, stirred the pot a lot more and served his notice to WFSB and suited up as an 'SPNaut.

Ken Boudreau and Rymanowski were refugees from WHCT Channel 18, the 1950s CBS pay-per-view experiment that became a low-power over-the-air pulpit for evangelists and then a failing independent channel.

I can recall Bobby Schlenker as one of the earliest FSB defectors, setting up a two-inch videotape machine in Scott Rasmussen's condo in Farmington Woods to edit some of the prelaunch promo events. The unwieldy machines were thought to be too heavy for the United Cable attic flooring.

Schlenker went on to ABC before it was part of the ESPN tree and worked with Barbara Walters and *20/20*, the mama network's version of *60 Minutes*.

Eno and Weed, inseparable pals, led ESPN editing crews, Eno moving on to an active political life as first selectman of Old Lyme, Connecticut, and Weed to a much too early repose.

Chuck said "having Steve Myers join us was a blessing. The farm was being run by children and the company needed an experienced mature cog in the engine. Most important was Steve's mentoring ability for young folks and me."

The bond Steve Myers developed with his tech staff is evidenced by the pranks they'd play on him. One went awry, as told by **Dave Overson,** the WDRC radio production superstar who became an 'SPNaut:

It was Christmas time at ESPN 1980.

I walked into the engineering maintenance area and came upon a couple of the engineers working on a box. Inside the box was an inflatable sex doll hooked up to a small CO_2 canister.

The guys had rigged the box, so when you open the box the sex doll would inflate and come out of the box. I said who is this for? The guys said it was a Christmas present for Steve Myers.

We all laughed for a bit. Then one of the guys asked, "How can we get this to him without him seeing it?"

One of the guys jumped right in and said, "I know where Steve's daughter lives. Dave and I can drop it off at her house." So all of us wrapped the box in nice Christmas wrappings. It looked terrific. Later that evening on our way home, we stopped by Steve's daughter's house and delivered the box.

We told her it was from the engineering department at ESPN. This was three days before Christmas and on the box we wrote DO NOT OPEN UNTIL CHRISTMAS . . .

Two days after Christmas, all the daytime engineers were called to the maintenance room. When we walked in, there was Steve Myers standing there with a scowl on his face. We all thought "Oh boy, we are screwed now."

Steve began to laugh and thanked all of us for the wonderful Christmas present. Steve added though, it would have been better to open the present without my grandson in the room.

All of us had the deer in the headlights look. Then Steve laughed.

He said his grandson asked him if this was his girlfriend.

We all broke up. This is what it was like in the very early days at ESPN.

Ken Boudreau and **Jeff Israel** had long careers at ESPN, Boudreau eventually becoming senior director of media assets.

Israel's broad talents ended up positioning him as a technical leader in electronic news gathering, studio, and electronic field production roles before answering a call to become president of Temple Sinai in nearby Newington, Connecticut. Jeff is an advocate for Voices of Hope, the organization of Holocaust survivors' descendants dedicated to sharing the experiences of the survivors for the benefit of future generations.

Frank Pingree, another technical 'SPNaut, was in great demand in those earliest days, as his deep voice was regularly recruited to speak the brought-to-you-by billboards at the beginning of programs. Described as bringing his vocal cords to work in a wheelbarrow, Pingree emigrated from radio station WKSS.

Another emigré, **Colin Fox**, was a United Cable tech, recruited to serve as minder of satellite connections, especially at that jitter-filled moment on September 7, 1979.

Production Team

When Stu Evey and Getty money shanghaied Simmons and Connal, it didn't take long for Scotty to get moving by assembling a team of a half-dozen producer/directors and supporting production assistants. That team of Connal-recruited producer/directors star in the *SportsCenter* chapter, chapter 5.

Bob Pronovost

One personality, Bob Pronovost, counts among the early "who knew" collection for a few important reasons, not the least of which was we were housemates and softball teammates while we worked for Hartford's CBS affiliate, WFSB. We are friends.

The house we shared was amazing. It sat on top of Avon Mountain in Connecticut and was one of a collection of homes owned by Gore Vidal's stepmother, Kit, who would only rent to bachelors. We shared it with another WFSB gent, the stylish Jay Goshen, who died of cancer while we were together.

Before Jay passed, the Parsonage, as our lair was called, became party headquarters, replete with its own police force, a state trooper who lived in an apartment at the mountaintop tower, the site of Connecticut State Police communication antennae and equipment. He, a bachelor too, enjoyed our parties and provided some other protections as we bumped against traffic regulations.

THE PARSONAGE
COURTESY SCOTT CHARETTE

Bob, of course was part of the production team I put together for those 1978 ESPN sample telecasts at the University of Connecticut. He and his mentor Jim Stewart led that team.

Often we'd commute together, and those mornings Bob would be full of TV production wisdom or depression, depending on how his favorite sports teams did overnight. More on that and the production team in the *SportsCenter* chapter.

After my ESPN experience, Bob, Jim Stewart, and I combined to launch WTIC Channel 61, with former president Jimmy Carter, braving a teleprompter breakdown and making sure the dedication went smoothly. Along with the former president, we were a tight team.

FANS IN THE STANDS

Revolution has role players. In the ESPN birthing story many nursed us through the gestation period that began shortly after Bill and Scott Rasmussen spent a late night drawing on a yellow legal pad the design for the Bristol building that put ESPN into millions of households, and hundreds of countries.

More Rasmussen notes, scripting, and on-paper needs ended up in the earliest hands of an ESPN cheerleader, and adjunct messaging developer, printing impresario, and frequently and mischievously coarse non vivant, Guy Wilson.

Guy Wilson

Guy Wilson was the hands-on owner of Connecticut Lithographics who adopted ESPN as his pet project. His trademark raucous and off-color sense of humor was ineffable, as was his great eye for layout and design.

Taken much too young, Guy Wilson advised deep-sixing the clunky E.S.P. Network logo and replacing it wih a more prominent and streamlined typeface, combining the full ESPN acronym.

It was Guy who recommended (and we accepted) Futura ND Display as the font that brought ESPN's founding messages to the public.

And it was Guy Wilson who when he heard me tell of Bill Rasmussen's trip to Getty Oil to seal the investment deal who designed, before my very eyes, the orange oval to surround the acronym.

Guy likened the oval to the logos of other prominent oil companies, such as Esso, Amoco, and STP, adding orange as Getty's preference. Guy Wilson's faith in the all-sports television dream was a constant source of encouragement for many of us early flyers.

John Toner

John Toner was the athletic director of the University of Connecticut and a very early influencer in the ESPN success story. Significantly, he was

ORIGINAL ESPN LOGO

ESPN SECOND LOGO WITH OVAL

next in line to become the president of the NCAA as 'SPNnauts began to lift off.

He paved the way, inviting our presentations to NCAA's TV hierarchy, a virtual fiefdom run by Navy athletic director Captain Bo Coppedge who, once activated by John Toner, got on the ESPN team and steered us through the NCAA labyrinth.

Without John Toner's qualified introduction and pending power seat, the NCAA/ESPN alliance would have been arduous if at all successful. Toner also set up a program of University of Connecticut sports events that we televised as proof of concept demonstrations to the cable, advertising, and money markets.

At the time Toner was helping get the NCAA/ESPN alliance started, the National Invitational Tournament (NIT) at Madison Square Garden dominated and the NCAA National Championship was conducted in its shadow. The influential shift began when ESPN began its wall-to-wall coverage of the NCAA tournament, now the blockbuster March Madness Road to the Final Four that has relegated NIT to an also-ran status.

Joe Soltys

UConn's enthusiasm for ESPN's prospects was also supported by the university's sports information director, Joseph Soltys. His support was not unfamiliar.

Years earlier Joe mentored me, a rookie sportswriting assistant, in an informal tutelage, setting a soft set of do's and don'ts in the big-time press boxes of the college stadia and field houses.

As UConn demonstration telecasts showed cable giants there was a sports tsunami coming, Joe Soltys quietly made the first wave possible, accommodating our ever-present production crew and equipment.

Ray Maher

Ray Maher was a competitor, confederate, and cohort of mine during our mutual heydays in the stuffy Hartford advertising community where we both stood out as Peck's bad boy types, though as leaders in the local ad industry's long-overdue creative insurrection.

We'd beat on each other competing for clients and then find a way to wear jeans in the hallowed halls of America's Insurance City. Then we might 420 lace our cocktail hours, backslapping along the way.

When I visited Ray Maher's offices in an ESPN capacity it was early November 1978. I poured a flagon full of all-sports television visions to Ray, and told him I didn't like the name and hoped he'd help me pitch to change it to IBC, standing for International Broadcasting Company.

Sure enough, Ray delivered speculatively an array of IBC visuals capable of de-socking Don Draper. That must have been around mid-November, because I scheduled an all-hands meeting to consider the drastic change I proposed.

I believed that to play in the TV network big league we needed a three-letter acronym like NBC, ABC, and CBS. Moreover ours should include the letters B and C, hence: IBC.

Prior to the meeting to pitch the major change, we launched our November 17 demonstration telecast which begat a snippet of a story in *Sports Illustrated*, which headlined our ESP Network name, and all hell broke loose after that.

The flurry of attention that the *SI* story triggered was poison to IBC and the plot that Ray had so carefully executed was executed. In its wake I kept the storyboards and logos for a long time, as a touchable artifact of what should have been. If I could find Ray, I'd honor him with an 'SPNaut tribute, though I wonder if he'd be pissed if I did. Maybe.

Meredith Downey

Mrs. Downey is an artist of compelling talent who over time has answered ridiculous calls by me to help produce a prop or a costume. Her creative hands would design, sew, knit, and crochet some really advanced pieces.

Two that are firmly entrenched as favorites are the hand-stitched ESPN logo on a white golf shirt I wore the day I expected to be named *SportsCenter* chief producer, but wasn't. The other is the massive, beautiful ESPN banner, a rich red corduroy with our oval logo in white.

That banner went to Louisville to videotape an American Slow Pitch Softball League game between the Kentucky Bourbon and Trenton Statesmen, including monster hitters and big leaguers who'd seen better days including former Yankee Joe Pepitone playing first base for Trenton.

The league was so unprepared for our cameras that Jim Stewart and I had to insist that a hole be cut in the behind-home-plate screen so our principal camera had a clear view of the entire field.

Knowing most of the hitters would be right-handed and blasting homers over the left field fence, I adroitly hung Meredith's banner on the left field wall, so it would be shown over and over again as home-run shots flew over it.

During the postgame atta-boys, good show, and thank you time with the pickup crew Jim had assembled from Louisville media friends, I turned to retrieve Meredith's masterpiece, and it was gone.

Really gone. Stolen gone. My heart sunk and has stayed there as I write about it.

Ray Smith

Ray Smith, it turns out, influenced my 35-plus years of sobriety and I am eternally grateful, though that influence was deadly to Ray.

He owned and operated the White Birch Inn, also known casually as Hamps; that nickname's origin is somewhere in the ether.

If you were going to lunch in the large formal dining area you'd be at the White Birch. If you were in the cozy bar where fish stories weren't the only exaggerations you were at Hamps.

However, 'SPNauts had a nickname of their own for Hamps. We called it Edit 3. We had two at HQ.

When making a first journey to inspect the site where the Getty dollars would enable the building of our studio and offices I, of course, had to inspect Hamps.

During inspection I met this gruff older dude, Ray Smith. It wasn't long, probably libation number two or three, that we mutually identified and bonded. When he poured an on-the-house fourth, we got down to business.

Ray wanted to know about this TV stuff that was going in down the street. So, I introduced him to the dream and he became a believer and a big-time benefactor. Moreover, Ray became a friend, an ear, and a voice that invariably erupted in a wizened streetwise wisdom that was easy to misjudge if you didn't listen with streetwise ears.

Sometimes after the late-night *SportsCenter* we'd close the joint and have raging games of setback. One dawn cracking, Ray took the card game to the wooded bowels of central Connecticut to a steam bath built over a huge boulder that was kept hot with ovens carved into it. The scene, to us card-playing rookies, was out of a B movie, replete with a muscular giant masseuse who not quite painfully whipped my bare butt with some sort of leaves on a branch.

Ray was such an ESPN fan that he lusted for one of the bright red nylon jackets that we gave to our production folks who were seen at events we televised. So, I got one for him.

Just my luck as I sauntered through the door one Saturday afternoon, calling to Ray to come and get the jacket that I'd lifted from supplies, Chet Simmons and Scotty Connal were having a casual lunch in one of Hamps's booths to witness the gift giving.

It was another one of those "shouldn't have done that moments" that didn't endear me to the new bosses. They added up, as my gallows humor wasn't as appreciated in this new environment as it was in the newsrooms I cut my media teeth in.

Our daily shenanigans waned as Ray began to feel the expanding effects of his liver. Our friendship didn't and when the Duke of Hamps was finally reluctantly, hospitalized with severe implications, I made it to Bristol Hospital to visit my friend.

So quickly had latent cirrhosis erupted that Ray lay helpless, jaundiced, bloated, and grouchy. As more folks began to crowd our intimate time, I excused myself, walking toward the corridor.

Nearly escaping, a familiar "Hey!" stopped me cold. I turned around and looked at Ray. He pointed his fat index finger at me and said: "Don't ever let this happen to you!"

From that moment a blurry recollection of the scene sat in my subconscious, until truly fearing the same predicament I surrendered and began a nearly decade-long fight with booze, winning some, losing many until on May 21, 1987 on the last stool in Ted Turner's familiar Newport Black Pearl, I had my last drink.

Thanks, Ray. So far it hasn't happened to me. I'm sorry it happened to you.

The Black Pearl
REPRINTED BY PERMISSION OF THE RAY ELLIS GALLERY

THE 'SPNaut TATTOO AND GROUND CONTROL ORDER OF THE ORANGE OVAL TEMPLATES

The imaginary 'SPNaut tattoo was applied to '78 and '79er friends and colleagues only when this author's octogenarian memory was able. For those 'SPNauts that are hiding in a hippocampus fold, I ask forgiveness and empathy.

'SPNaut 'SPNaut
1978   1979

The Ground Control Order of the Orange Oval is hereby authorized to be worn by Ground Control supporters of 'SPNauts who worked in the nascent days of the network with dedication and enthusiasm on a par with the high flyers named above. The 'SPNaut Ground Control Team is a concoction of the author. Its membership is comprised of support personnel and the millions of sports fans everywhere entitled to wear the coveted Orange Oval.

Some of our figurative art should be offered to the progeny of those sports television visionaries who left us much too early for our liking.

For those of us just hiding in plain sight, I tell our stories with a Vaselined lens.

CHAPTER 2

Of Course We Can

TWO NEWSPAPER GUYS AND A RADIO VETERAN PUT ESPN'S FIRST PRO-
grams on the air.

While Bill and Scott Rasmussen and J. B. Doherty traipsed around
America pitching the brash all-sports television dream to cable, money,
NCAA, and advertising bishops, it fell on the shoulders of three of us in
Connecticut to produce live show-and-tell sports events via satellite so
Bill and J. B. could schmooze those key mini audiences.

Of the three of us, Lou Palmer, Dennis Randall, and me, Lou's live
broadcasting experiences led the way. Dennis and I, escapees from the
crumbling glory of the *Hartford Times*, had touched the magic of radio
with pictures, just enough to know the ESPN dream could come true.

At the office Scott, Ed, and Jim Bates telephone corralled cable companies to put our demonstration event on their systems, and to this day
none of us know how many saw the semi-grand debut of ESP Network
on the evening of November 17, 1978.

So, there we three were, at the University of Connecticut, with a
rented remote truck and crew from Telfax in Philadelphia to truly nar-
rowcast a basketball game between UConn's men's team and Athletes in
Action, a touring team promoting Christian values.

Lou recruited a former colleague, Arnold Dean, to support Lou's
flawless play-by-play with color commentary. Dennis and I were in the
Telfax truck, I as alleged producer and Dennis operating the on-screen
title messaging we rookies learned was called a character generator.

In a weak attempt to humor-wash our inability to afford a then quite costly instant replay contraption, I hired Phyllis Kommoner, known as the world's fastest cartoonist. She sat courtside and drew images of on-court action as the world's slowest instant replay.

Though four decades of braggadocio has ensued, it has also served to put some soft-viewing Vaseline on the memory lens of the thrilling debut weekend of ESPN. Some unforgettable recollections include:

- the blood draining from my face when the Telfax-provided director leapt from the remote truck during halftime to deal with a gastrointestinal attack. He returned as the pretaped interview with UConn's John Toner was ending. Whew!

- later, as we were moving equipment for the next morning's soccer telecast, gastro comeuppance bent me over in spasm caused by the two or three rolls of Life Savers I nervously consumed during the live debut as oral camouflage for surreptitious vodka sipping.

- the $5,000 bouncing check I wrote to New York's Dolphin Productions to produce the computer animation introduction to ESPNetwork's debut programming, because they wouldn't let the animation out of their studios without payment. It was covered, barely.

- the admiration for Lou Palmer's versatility as he teamed with Seamus Malin, the Harvard footballer and experienced soccer on-air analyst to guide us through the sport yet to gain media popularity stateside.

- the faux advertising we ran consisting of commercials I had produced for clients like Waldenbooks stores and United Technologies, and one Mary Walton and I shot for former UConn basketball star Bob Haines, a developer who paid me by allowing residence in one of his Farmington Woods managed housing projects. It made us look like an actual entity.

The debut weekend started winter through spring periodic satellite-fed cablecasts, predicting the sports television tsunami that would fully launch on September 7, 1979. The UConn demonstration package included more basketball and soccer, indoor track and field, women's gymnastics, lacrosse, field hockey, and baseball.

With the imprimatur of John Toner at the highest level and Joe Soltys on the ground, our fledgling satellite-fed, sportscasting barrier-busting dream team carried on through the winter and spring almost becoming a fixture on the Storrs Connecticut campus.

For Joe and me it was a mentoring mirror, reflecting how nearly two decades earlier he showed this sportswriting puppy how press box protocol worked and how not to prove I was a real rookie. That personal relationship with Joe became ESPN generational when a summer later, Joe's son Mike began as an intern and 43 years later retired as ESPN's communications vice president.

On that occasion **Mike Soltys** was invited to contribute this memory:

After Bill Rasmussen was fired by Colleen Howe Memorial Day weekend of 1978 from the New England Whalers, he immediately began brainstorming his next move with an eye on sports media.

Among the recipients of a summer call was my dad, Joseph Soltys, who Bill had known since the mid-1960s when Bill was calling UMass games on radio and Dad was in the midst of a 25-year career as the sports information director at rival UConn. Bill originally was interested in presenting a package of UConn games to the state of Connecticut cable systems, but as we now know over that summer his ambitions grew. Dad's role was to facilitate a meeting with UConn athletic director John Toner (who fortuitously for the future of ESPN was on path to become president of the NCAA) and do some follow-up after those meetings.

That follow-up included issuing a press release September 25, 1978 announcing a partnership between UConn and "ESP-TV of Plainville" which offered an $18 subscription for 35 sporting events. No money was ever collected for the "UConn Sports Package" and it was converted into a series of "demo events" in the lead-up to the launch of ESPN. The first demo event was November 17, 1978 when the UConn basketball team, in its final season before joining the Big East, hosted Athletes in Action in an exhibition game at the Field House.

Two summers later, as a 20-year-old heading into my senior year at UConn, I was the passenger in my dad's car as he pulled into a lot behind the Field House. In an oddity tied to UConn's roots as an agriculture school, the SID office was in the agriculture building but his mail was delivered to the athletic department, necessitating a daily visit. It was an oddity that launched my career.

"There is Bill Rasmussen," Dad pointed out. "You should ask him if he needs an intern." After introductions, I told Bill what he has long called "the magic words": "I will work for free." On the spot I became Bill's first intern and when he returned to Bristol he told his new head of communications, Rosa Gatti, that she could have a free intern if she was interested. Fortunately, she was and my 43-year relationship with Bill, Rosa, Rosa's right-hand man Chris LaPlaca, and ESPN began.

Over the next 43 years in the Communications Department at ESPN I had a front-row seat to the greatest business success story in sports history. I have countless memories and friendships with my talented colleagues who built the company and the media that chronicled it. And along the way, until my retirement from ESPN in June 2023, I became an ESPN historian and a go-to source on what happened and when.

I am eternally grateful to my dad for many things, including his relationship with a fired friend who would launch an extraordinary company in the middle of my home state.

Telfax had a calendar filled with prior commitments, as they were the production subsidiary of the Philadelphia Spectrum where the NHL Flyers and NBA Sixers monopolized their availability. They referred us to WHYY Channel 56, the Philadelphia PBS station that had a production truck we could rent.

As it turned out, the truck and its skeleton crew led by the eye-twinkling, chain-smoking, get-it-done engineering chief Keith Schermerhorn who brought the truck to UConn stayed with us throughout the spring and heroically became ESPN's actual master control room when it went on the air full-time in September. The public and contracted full-time production date was firmly committed, but the construction of the ESPN headquarters missed that deadline by a lot and Keith's team, later led by John Collins, parked alongside the unfinished studio on cinder blocks, so it wouldn't sink in the mud . . . but it leaned slightly, unnerving crews. That was a lesson learned as the WHYY big boy did sink up to its axles while it waited patiently behind the home plate screen for the UConn baseball games it was to produce during a rainy springtime. After rescue operations that included monster tow trucks, the games played on as did ESP Network, innovating in the vacuum of satellite-fed regulations.

One innovative backfire was attaching a microphone to UConn's coach Larry Panciera. Larry, a college coaching baseball biggie, was cut from the pre–bubble gum baseball mold. The sound of regular tobacco expectorations punctuating our baseball ambience was a bit much and got shut down after the first base line camera caught Coach Panciera in the act, explaining the disgusting sound that permeated the first inning.

Jim Stewart, the meticulously presented, every-hair-in-place director, longtime friend, and former CBS affiliate colleague had to have a long drink of water after that image, which did not get replayed, though saved to a long-gone blooper reel.

In the annals of early ESPN, Jim Stewart should get more credit than he does in other recollections, because it was he that Lou Palmer and I relied upon to put a full crew of freelancing television veterans together to support Keith's skeleton staff in the remote truck. Many freelanced from Jim's staff at the WFSB CBS affiliate and *Post-Newsweek* property. Their off-the-clock moonlighting for us ultimately led to the exodus to ESPN by a bunch of their talent, pissing off management there.

One of my favorite moments during the UConn sample ESPN telecasts was seeing John Robella overseeing the movement of our signals via Southern New England Telephone microwave to relay points that would eventually get our images to a Satcom I uplink to spread ESPN across North America. I'd always secretly hoped that John might talk about my "big deal" in our hometown, as he and I were both educated in a system that in 1960 and 1961 respectively graduated fewer than 150 students from the WPA-built Griswold High School. He was still in town, and I had moved along geographically.

Joining the WFSB exodus to ESPN were notable talents such as Jerry Weed, Ralph Eno, Tony Valentino, and a trio of admins from their sales and marketing departments, not to mention directing prodigy Bob Pronovost. It served as tat to the tit serendipitously shot at the WFSB general manager who stopped underwriting my budget there to teach the city's largest advertisers how to create effective television advertising.

We produced lacrosse at Yale, more Big East basketball, soccer, and a women's gymnastics triangular meet at UConn with Bridgewater State and Yale providing the competition. It turned into a production fiasco, a live event that almost crashed before it began.

Our fledgling network had no contingency programming on deck when Bridgewater State's coach, Alice Gonsalves, was surprised by the presence of our live cameras and refused to compete fearing the televised exposure of the thick-in-the-thigh spandex-clad competitors.

An in-the-moment détente was reached when we promised not to show the women in question, though it made for some confusing watching.

Live TV is a character builder, an adrenaline-producing addictive.

CHAPTER 3

By George

"BY GEORGE! I THINK HE'S GOT IT!"

That old English oath is a phrase of admiration and approval often used to express surprise or joy at an achievement.

Well, by George, I think our George has got it, in terms of an authentic inside story of ESPN's earliest days, from the unique perspective of the protector of Getty Oil's investment, a scary endeavor to some of their conservative oilmen.

George Conner was the direct opposite of his swashbuckling, visionary, bloviating, liquid boss, Stu Evey, who was in charge of Getty investments that were not pumped out of the ground. Without Evey's sponsorship inside of Getty there would be no ESPN. As Evey's assistant, George Conner was privy to the germination of Getty's investment of millions that made ESPN possible.

Without George Conner's everyday, on-site, shirtsleeves-rolled, enthusiastic, and sometime financial daredevil acts, the chaos that comprised the months leading up to the ESPN launch would have been intolerable. As much as Evey wanted to play TV mogul during ESPN's birthing cramps, he was also constrained by duties in Los Angeles, often at Santa Anita racetrack with his brother in barleycorn John Forsythe and their equine investment Bold Mamselle. George E. Conner, formally, Finance Manager, Diversified Operations, Getty Oil Company Vice President, Corporate Finance, ESPN, was and is officially the direct opposite of his boss, a friendly, steady, talented, proud professional who ultimately loved ESPN so much that when his stint with us was over, he didn't want to do much else.

One day after a short period back at LA Getty, George walked into Evey's office and resigned, telling Evey he was going to take a year off. It turned into five years in his Marina Del Ray beach house where he'd often wave at neighbors Susan Anton and Dudley Moore.

George told me "nothing could be as exciting as what we did," adding "I wouldn't trade that ESPN experience for anything in the world." "I do think about ESPN several times every day," he smiles.

George's ESPN fervor doesn't waver as is evidenced by the prominent display of the employee-signed banner framed and gifted George when he left Bristol. It hangs in his home in Tulsa, Oklahoma, where he returned after the one-year beach sabbatical that turned into five years.

George's roots are in Oklahoma. George's parents operated the Coca-Cola franchise in McAlester, his mom serving in that role until she was 79 and lived to 101, so his roots are as deep as his genes are good.

George Conner with his prized autographed ESPN banner
PHOTO COURTESY WHITNEY UPTON

Mentioned elsewhere herein is the most authentic recounting of ESPN's birthing from Bill Rasmussen's perspective, his diary-like *Sports Junkies Rejoice.* Here is the other authentic diary-like perspective from George Conner, nearly of equal value to Bill's though not as chronological. George Conner's value to ESPN's birth cannot be understated.

So, By George, here is how he saw it:

Early December, 1978

During my tenure as finance manager for the non-oil division of Getty Oil Company in Los Angeles, California, our responsibilities included overseeing the Getty Museum in Malibu, the vineyards in the Bakersfield area, and company cars, among other things. When individuals approached Getty with their innovative ideas for utilizing our funds, our division evaluated many of those proposals.

I had recently returned from Hawaii with my boss, Stuart Evey (a top executive at Getty), where we were considering the purchase of the Kona Surf Hotel properties. We had plans to collaborate with Jack Nicklaus to construct a second 18-hole golf course on the properties once the acquisition was finalized. Nicklaus was partnering with the venture capital firm K.S. Sweet, based in Pennsylvania. At Getty Oil Company, our word was as binding as a written contract. We had already agreed on the purchase price for the properties. However, the sellers learned about our intentions to involve Nicklaus and significantly raised the selling price out of greed. I advised Stu that the new price wasn't justified for us to proceed.

The following morning after returning to LA, Stu summoned me to his office around 9 a.m. He had just concluded a discussion with Bill Rasmussen from Connecticut regarding an intriguing venture. Stu handed me a 20-page proposal encased in a clear plastic cover. He mentioned he would call me in the mid-afternoon to hear my thoughts. Returning to my office, I informed Janet, my secretary, that Stu was quite enthusiastic about this venture and probably wouldn't wait until the middle of the afternoon for my input. As expected, he reached out to me around 11:45 a.m. and suggested we meet in the lounge atop our Getty Building. Stu was enjoying a scotch and water, while I opted for a rum and Coca-Cola.

Stu inquired about my impressions of the project. I informed him that it seemed interesting and warranted further exploration. However, he revealed a challenge: Bill needed a response within three weeks (by December 31st).

Bill had reached his credit limit on all his credit cards, the venture capital firm (K.S. Sweet in King of Prussia, Pennsylvania) had already advanced around $125,000, and the bank had declined further assistance. After receiving rejections from seven other major corporations, Bill turned to Getty Oil on the recommendation of K.S. Sweet. Though I believed that agreeing to a project of this magnitude within three weeks was impossible for Getty Oil, I suggested we might at least provide a definitive answer. Stu instructed me to commence the evaluation process, referring to me as his "due-diligence guru," a title he bestowed on me in his book about ESPN.

Mr. Rasmussen was requesting from Getty Oil what he had previously requested from seven other companies, all of whom had declined. K.S. Sweet suggested that Bill approach Getty Oil after his previous attempts were unsuccessful. His vision involved establishing television studios in Bristol, CT. While I knew the location of Connecticut, I was initially unaware of Bristol's location. He aimed to acquire broadcasting rights from the NCAA, procure state-of-the-art (expensive) television trucks, hire costly on-air talent, lease premium time on RCA's new satellite, and broadcast sports content 24/7. He was seeking $10 million for this venture—an impressive sum for that era, equivalent to around $47 million in 2023.

I traveled to Chicago to meet Bill Rasmussen for the first time. I also consulted with a professor knowledgeable about the emerging cable industry. However, it became apparent that Mr. Rasmussen possessed a more advanced understanding of the landscape. My interactions with Bill left me impressed.

Over the following weeks, I conversed with Bill on most days from various locations across the United States, often using pay phones or available office spaces. These conversations included meetings with RCA Americom (the company housing the satellite for the proposed TV programming), the NCAA Television Committee in Kansas City (discussions about broadcasting NCAA college events), and cable company executives. Simultaneously, I collaborated with Scott Rasmussen, Bill's son, to analyze financial projections for the prospective 24/7 sports television network.

During this three-week evaluation while traveling around the country, I seized opportunities to gather input. In restaurants and bars, I would inquire with ladies about their potential interest in watching women's tennis events on a new television network we were considering launching. Notably, women's tennis events were not televised at that time. The feedback I received was predominantly positive.

In a serendipitous turn, my childhood friend who worked at a Dallas television station proved to be valuable. Attending Dallas Cowboy games and events afforded me valuable insights. During December 1978, the Dallas Cowboys and Los Angeles Rams had a playoff game in LA. My friend invited me to a pregame party. There, I had the chance to converse with Tex Schramm, the manager of the Dallas Cowboys. I informed him about the proposal to establish a 24/7 cable network dedicated to broadcasting sports. While most individuals were receptive, Schramm expressed skepticism. He highlighted the existing sports content on television and questioned the feasibility of Rasmussen's idea. His perspective contrasted with the majority who supported Rasmussen's vision.

December 31, 1978, Tulsa, Oklahoma

Midmorning Tulsa Time—I am at my good friend Andrea Nielsen's house in Tulsa. Stu calls and asks me what I think about Bill Rasmussen's idea of 24/7 sports on television. I tell him, "If Bill needs an answer today, we have to tell him 'No!' But I like the idea and think you do too, so why don't we advance him enough money for payroll and other expenses until we can finish our evaluation?" (His payroll was for eight people; he had to make a $35,000 payment to RCA Americom for one month's lease on the satellite the next day.) At Getty Oil Company, we sometimes drilled dry holes that cost much more than this!

Later that day, Bill called Mr. Evey. "Have you had a chance to look at my idea?" Mr. Evey's response was, "Yes, we have, Bill. And if you have to have an answer today, it is NO!" Long pause, then, "If you want, we will advance you enough money for payroll and other expenses until we can finish evaluating your project." Bill says, "That sounds pretty good, Mr. Evey." Then Stu says, "Bill, just work through George, and we will go from there."

From that moment on, for the next three and a half years, the only thing I worked on was helping to get ESPN on the air. I had told Getty the only way I was recommending it was if we used only the highest quality people and equipment, as most new businesses did not succeed. And that is what we did!

March 1979 / First Day in Connecticut / Connecticut State Police—All Points Bulletin for Pickup of George's Hertz Rental Car Used in Armed Robbery!

"The Man from Getty"—that is what a lot of ESPN employees referred to me as over the three and a half years I was there.

Getty assigned me to go to Connecticut to further evaluate the ESPN Project. I arrived late in the day at Bradley International Airport, near Hartford, rented a Hertz, and drove to the Holiday Inn in Plainville. At that time, Bill and his eight employees were renting space from the local Plainville cable system. The next morning, I went to the motel front desk to check out. The gentleman at the desk pulled my charge folio, looked down at it, then back up at me several times without saying a word. He looked over to his right at the lady on the switchboard and back down at the folio that had a pink note attached. Being in a hurry to get checked out and on to meet the ESPN staff, I then said, "I am in a hurry, what is the problem?" He said, "This note says, 'may be driving a stolen car!'"

At that moment, the lady (motel manager) had finished her call on the switchboard. She said, "Mr. Conner, everything is okay; however, around midnight last night there was an armed robbery at the service station here. There was an all-points alert to stop a car with license plates that matched my Hertz rental." She said the Connecticut State Police had my room surrounded inside and outside by the window and were getting ready to break the door down when one of the troopers noted that the front license plate had been removed from the front of my rental. They halted the storming of my hotel room after figuring I was probably not the armed robber! She said the head of the Connecticut State Police wanted to talk to me, and she got him on the phone. He told me they had talked to Hertz and he wanted me to take my rental back to Bradley International and get another car. He did not want me to go on the interstate and gave me backroad directions to the airport, telling me, if I got stopped, to hold my hands up and not move!

In my new Hertz rental, I arrived at the ESPN office a bit late!

Scott Rasmussen—Cofounder of ESPN

Scott confessed to me: In the early days, when they would go to lunch, they would leave the phone off the hook so people calling would get a busy signal. This let them think lots was going on at ESP Network!

In the first few weeks I was at ESP Network, as it was called at that time, when people called information for our phone number, the operator would often say, "ESP What!" It didn't take them long to know what ESPN was.

NCAA Television Committee Meeting in Kansas City

Bill wanted me to attend a meeting in Kansas City with the NCAA Television Committee, who were deciding whom to give the television rights *to for their college games. I think there were maybe two other groups wanting those rights in addition to Bill. The committee was a who's who of college coaches (Darrell Royal, University of Texas; Eddie Crowder, University of Colorado, and several more). I was there with Bill and J. B. Doherty from K.S. Sweet, who had advanced some early seed money to ESP Network but had said no more! Bill introduced me as George Conner from Getty Oil Company, Los Angeles. That's all he said! Later, Walter Byers, chairman, asked Bill, "Bill, if we give you the rights, how do we know you have the money to pay?" Bill immediately said, "Mr. Byers, give us the bank account number and we will wire the money!" J. B. was sitting right next to me. I heard him gulp and turn beet red, as he knew they were not advancing any more money and knew Getty Oil had not made any commitment at that point. He also knew Bill was up to his limit on all his credit cards, and the bank had said no more money!*

ESPN People Stories

One of my favorite memories about ESPN is its people. People arrived at our offices every day to apply for jobs! One of those was George Bodenheimer. We hired him. That night, he called his dad, a prominent attorney in Hartford. He said, "Dad, Good News! Bad News! I HAVE A JOB AT ESPN! BUT it's in the Mail Room!" We hired George at the lowest pay we had at the time. The "Mail Room" was a very small closet.

George would take my company car to the Hartford airport to pick up my boss from Getty Oil when he visited Bristol. Over the years, George advanced in a number of ESPN jobs and became our longest-serving president.

Hiring Rick Barry

I hired Richard B. (Rick) Barry to help me in the Finance Department. He had been working for Hartford Insurance in Hartford, CT. At ESPN, new hires had to get up to speed very fast, as everything at ESPN was moving at lightning speed. After Rick had been working there for a few weeks, I told my good friend Andrea Nielsen, "I'm not sure Rick is going to work out; things at Hartford Insurance went a lot slower than what's happening at ESPN."

Rick became my "right-hand" person soon after that! He did a great job, and we became good friends! Rick went on to become a senior vice president at ESPN with a very big budget responsibility!

More about People

I attribute a lot of ESPN's success to Chester Simmons, ESPN president, who previously was head of NBC Sports. I liked Chet! He brought in some very talented personnel who met my requirement that we had to have the very best people to succeed!

Allan (Scotty) Connal from NBC Sports was responsible for our high-quality broadcasts. Really liked Scotty! I went up to his office one morning around 1 a.m.; he had his feet up on his desk watching a hockey game! Chris Berman became a favorite of ESPN fans.

Unwinding after Work

The workdays were often long at ESPN. I would sometimes go to a favorite restaurant, Avon Old Farms Inn, in Avon, CT, to unwind. I'd have a rum and Coca-Cola at the bar, plan out my "To-Do" list on a yellow pad, and do a lot of thinking about what needed to be done. One day, I got a tap on my shoulder. It was Steve Bogart, who we had hired. He said, "George, would you like to come back and meet my mom?" What a thrill to get to meet Lauren Bacall, of Bogie and Bacall fame!

Getty Money

The Getty Oil Board of Directors met every three months. Before almost every board meeting during the three and a half years I was at ESPN, Stu Evey, my boss, would call me in Bristol. Our conversation would last about three minutes. Stu would say, "George, we are putting more money into this than you thought; is it going to go?" My reply: "Absolutely, Stu." I never wavered a second in that opinion! He would get us millions more until the next board meeting. We were spending lots of Getty's money!

National Cable Television Association Show in Las Vegas

May 20, 1979, Las Vegas: Our "booth" at the National Cable Television Show was one of our beautiful brand-new 18-wheeler state-of-the-art television production trucks. Ted Turner came up and said, "You guys are going to interview me! Where are you doing that?" I said, "Mr. Turner, we are set up on top of our new truck. I will hold the ladder for you." Mr. Turner said, "I'm not going to climb up that ladder!" I said, "Mr. Turner, this broadcast will be going around the world, and will be good for the news network you are going to launch!" I convinced him to climb onto our ESPN truck, and he was interviewed!

Media Stories

ESPN was receiving a lot of attention from the press, with coverage in the Wall Street Journal, Sports Illustrated, Hartford Courant, and more. Both my boss and Chet Simmons, who we hired from NBC Sports, had big egos. My boss, Stu Evey, called me several times after some stories were published, asking, "George, did you read that story in SI?" "No, I did not." "Why was my name not mentioned?" "I don't know, Stu, I didn't talk to the reporter."

One day, Bill walked over to my office and said, "Did you hear what Chet told our secretaries? He told our three secretaries, 'If a reporter shows up and wants to talk to Bill, tell them Bill is not available, but Chet is!'"

In my opinion, Bill was "the ESPN story," and the one the reporters wanted to speak with.

Call from Stu a Couple of Weeks Before Scheduled Launch

About two weeks before we had planned to go on the air with our first broadcast, Stu called me in Bristol. He said Chet had called him and claimed there was no way we would be ready by September 7, 1979. I assured Stu that Bill and I were confident we would be ready. Chet was not very happy when Stu told him we were going on the air on September 7 at 7 p.m. And we did! However, we had cut it quite close, perhaps less than 10 minutes! In those final moments before going live, we ran the cable from the SportsCenter set down the hall to a trailer behind the building so we could link to Satcom I, transponder #7.

Losing Sound Shortly after Launch

A large number of ESPN employees were at the Holiday Inn watching our first broadcast of SportsCenter. After the first SportsCenter, we switched to Boulder, Colorado, for an interview with Chuck Fairbanks, University of Colorado football coach. About 10 minutes into that interview, the TV lost all sound! I thought to myself, "Gosh! This is not how I wanted our first day to go!" It seemed like we had no sound for a long time. After we signed off for ESPN's first broadcast at 2 a.m., Bill, Scott, and I went into the control room and looked at the log. We had lost sound for about a minute!

Bill Rasmussen and Me

Bill has always given me a lot of credit for getting ESPN off the ground. I received the following text from Bill in December 2022, responding to a request that would have Bill introduce me to the current ESPN chairman Jimmy Pitaro.

"I expect he already knows, but I will certainly tell him of your impact on getting ESPN on the road to success. I still firmly believe: No George. No 'Gettysburg'—no $ hence, no ESPN. Bill."

By George, I think he got it.

CHAPTER 4

Flood the Zone

BY PUTTING A MEDIA GUY, AN ADMAN, TWO NEWSPAPER EDITORS, AND A promotion exec in the same room, a messaging explosion was bound to happen.

In many ways that's how ESPN became real. In any event, that's how we made it feel real in the consciousness of audiences we needed to reel into the all-sports television dream. It would be easy to label it smoke and mirrors, though through the combined creativity, vision, and experience of communicators talking about communication what was imagined all of a sudden started to make sense.

Starting with a press conference in Plainville with paltry attendance, a group of us that included Bill Rasmussen, Dennis Randall, Mike Caruso, John Foley, and me flooded the PR zone with so much information the weight of our PR releases defied getting spiked and ignored. Name-dropping, content predictions, and illustrations in lieu of photography were a staple of the 'SPNaut public relations machine that put a constant flow of "coming to a TV near you" in front of content-starved trade publications.

The vertical industry reporters and writers of mainstream media were afraid of being scooped in an era when morning edition competition counted, so breakthroughs in the *New York Times* and *LA Times* were not as hard as would-be PR vendors predicted. From the attic of our original Plainville offices our band of browbeaters led by Dennis were relentlessly making ESPN daydreams feel real already with stories that whet the appetites of sports fans and adjacent businesses. And when we'd get some actual news to promote, our team would be on it with headlines and copy that could stretch even a friendly editor's commitment to publish. After all how many readers, other than a few parents, might have jumped with glee when we shouted that ESPN would televise Pony League baseball's World Series?

Thankfully by the time of my swan-song production of All-Star NFL Arm Wrestling, Dennis, Mike, and John had left, and Rosa Gatti had taken the PR reins at ESPN and nary a word was written about it.

From the FAQ reproduced here to daily mailed and wired pro-nouncements, ESPN forced its way into the consciousness of industry and mass media.

We'd sketch our dreams with press releases showing fancy new headquarters and the fleet of remote production trucks we bragged that renowned Hollywood technical manufacturers Compact Video would build for us.

Even a wizened ol' sports editor's fancy would be caught with the Sputnik of all-sports television, so off to them went drawings of how our satellite-fed signals would begin. First we would mention our head-quarters replete with 10-meter parabolic earth receiving stations, and in the name-dropping spirit, to enliven interest and credibility, we would reference the building supervision by the Dale Eckert team that had built a studio for the Osmond musical family.

Days later came the story of our remote production fleet numbering seven to be stationed in key sports sections of America, able to produce a menu of live sports to be delivered all day, every day to hungry sports fans' appetites.

Not bashful, nor intimidated by practicalities, our press release machine would shout about anything new we were able to reel into the ESPN future, new major system operators, then a connected amalgama-tion of local cable systems.

The whales in that important segment of our future seemed to collect in Denver, so while our press release blitz softened up their awareness, our Johnny Appleseed, Bill Rasmussen, headed to Denver to plant the seeds.

The Entertainment and Sports Programming Network Inc.

ESPN FACTS

THE ENTERTAINMENT AND SPORTS PROGRAMMING NETWORK (ESPN) will begin full-time, all sports programming — highlighting National Collegiate Athletic Association (NCAA) events — on September 7 at 7 p.m. (EDT) as the first step in a plan to provide 24-hour programming of professional and amateur sports nationally and internationally.

ESPN's "NCAA SPORTS — The Championship Season" of NCAA events features championships in 11 Division I sports as well as 22 of 24 championship events in Divisions II and III. The several hundred-event series also includes participating NCAA college and conference regular-season competition in 18 sports.

Under the ESPN/NCAA agreement, ESPN coverage will be geographically balanced to include events in all parts of the United States.

ESPN was awarded a transponder by RCA on Satcom I in September of 1978. Satcom I is the domestic communications satellite being utilized by the cable television industry. ESPN took full-time service of Transponder #7 on Satcom I on January 1, 1979 and a second full-time transponder has been ordered from RCA.

In addition, the ESPN national headquarters building in Bristol, Ct., will be completed in September, 1979. The facility, being built under the direction of Dale C. Eckert of Los Angeles, will include complete and modern studios and a ten-meter transmit/receive earth station, provided by Scientific Atlanta of Atlanta, Ga., the country's major producer of satellite earth stations.

Seven remote facilities are being designed and furnished by Compact Video Systems, Inc., of Burbank, California.

ESPN PRESS-READY facts
COURTESY DENNIS RANDALL

We'd water their curiosity with a series of demonstration live televised events that I'd produce, mostly at UConn, but amazingly aimed at the smallest audience of influencers, the decision-makers in Denver, Greg Powers and Chip Morris of American Telecommunications, Gene Schneider of United Cable, and none other than the Cable Cowboy, John Malone of Tele-Communications, Inc., and his VP Graham Moors.

The Entertainment and Sports Programming Network Inc.

ESPN HEADQUARTERS

The Entertainment and Sports Programming Network is presently located in Plainville, Conn., but construction of the network's new headquarters in Bristol, Conn., is well underway and will be completed in September of 1979.

It is being built under the direction of the Dale C. Eckert Corporation of Riverside, Calif., the same company that put together the Osmond Studios in Provo, Utah. The new headquarters will house approximately 110 people by September.

ESPN's plant will include complete and modern studios and a ten-meter transmit/receive earth station provided by Scientific Atlanta of Atlanta, Ga., the country's major producer of satellite earth stations.

The earth station is the most sophisticated system available and will consist of two ten-meter, parabolic antennas which will provide total flexibility in transmitting and receiving.

ESPN's order — the first ever involving the installation of twin ten-meter antennas from the very beginning — is unique because provisions have been made for the new equipment to accommodate future advancements in satellite technology.

The earth stations in Bristol will be fully protected, meaning that there is a built-in backup for every major piece of equipment. This will insure cable systems operators uninterrupted programming at all times.

ESPN original headquarters illustration by G. G. Bray, AIA
COURTESY DENNIS RANDALL

As we pumped out these announcements, they became the pied pipers of our success, leading smaller companies to believe in our vision.

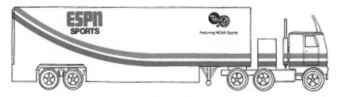

ESPN REMOTE FACILITIES

The Entertainment and Sports Programming Network will be televising sporting events, via satellite, from around the country beginning in September of 1979 and ESPN's fleet of seven ultra-modern, state-of-the-art remote units will be providing thousands of hours of sports programming.

Presently under construction by Compact Video Systems, Inc., of Burbank, Calif., two of the seven units will be on the road by September when ESPN's unique programming concept — highlighting a series of National Collegiate Athletic Association events in 18 sports — debuts with from 12 to 14 hours of sports daily.

The units will be furnished with the newest and most sophisticated equipment available to insure the highest quality transmission of sporting events possible. All ESPN programming will be sent to cable systems across the country through RCA's Satcom I, Transponder #7.

As well as providing the remote units for ESPN, Compact Video will also offer consulting services and assist in the construction of a broadcast studio at ESPN's new headquarters which are presently being built in Bristol, Conn.

In addition, Compact Video will aid in the hiring and training of technical personnel and in ESPN's use of certain production and post-production facilities owned by Compact.

ESPN remote broadcast trucks PR
COURTESY DENNIS RANDALL

And not to ignore the Madison Avenue crowd, we supported our ad guys by pummeling their inboxes with this announcement that the Big Apple's largest cable system would carry ESPN.

Our Selectrics would bang out no bigger story than the announcement that the NCAA had agreed to grant ESPN rights to televise its full array of championships and in-season sports that were not otherwise under contract. Even Saturday football could be aired on a delayed basis.

The Entertainment and Sports Programming Network Inc.
319 COOKE STREET □ PLAINVILLE, CONNECTICUT 06062 □ 203-747-6847

TCI TO CARRY
ESPN SPORTS

FOR IMMEDIATE RELEASE

PLAINVILLE, Conn. — Tele-Communications Inc., of Denver, Colo., the third largest Multiple System Operator (MSO) in the United States, has signed a letter of intent to carry sports programming provided by the Entertainment and Sports Programming Network.

The announcement was made by J. C. Sparkman, Vice-President and General Manager of TCI, and William F. Rasmussen, President of ESPN.

Tele-Communications Inc., has more than 700,000 subscribers in systems owned and managed by TCI in 32 states.

"We were favorably impressed and are very enthusiastic about ESPN's sports programming concept," said Sparkman. "We shook hands and will sign the final agreement soon."

ESPN will begin full-time, all-sports programming — highlighting a series of more than 350 NCAA events in 18 sports — in September of this year via RCA's Satcom I (Transponder #7) as the first step in a plan to provide 24-hour programming of professional and amateur sports nationally and internationally.

"Our meetings with TCI have been very successful," said Rasmussen, "and we're very happy to add TCI to our sports programming network."

-30-

CONTACT: DENNIS RANDALL (203) 747-6847

TCI PRESS-READY
COURTESY DENNIS RANDALL

What a coup. What a parlay. Getty Oil, NCAA, and Budweiser. No more smoke, nor mirrors.

With the conservative NCAA under our belts, more admired sports brands began to sign up with what Chet Simmons made sure we referenced as the Worldwide Leader in Sports, perhaps a stretch at the moment, but prescient and to me, a genius tactical land grab.

Monaco Tennis, Davis Cup Tennis, National Baseball Congress, and the Professional Bowlers Association were early joiners as were Top Rank

The Entertainment and Sports Programming Network Inc.
319 COOKE STREET □ PLAINVILLE, CONNECTICUT 06062 □ 203-747-6847

VISION CABLE COMMUNICATIONS
JOINS GROWING LIST
OF ESPN AFFILIATES

PLAINVILLE, Conn. — Vision Cable Communications, Inc., of New York City is the newest Multiple System Operator (MSO) to become an affiliate of the Entertainment and Sports Programming Network and will carry sports programming provided by ESPN beginning in September of this year.

Mike Wilner, Vice-President of Vision Cable Communications, Inc., and Ron Newman, Vice-President of ESPN, made the joint announcement.

Vision Cable Communications, Inc., is composed of 14 cable systems in five states — New Jersey, Pennsylvania, North Carolina, South Carolina and Louisiana — and is initially committing 60,000 of its 100,000 subscribers to the ESPN package and will commit the remaining 40,000 as soon as technically possible.

"We plan on expanding and will provide ESPN programming to all of our present and future subscribers, including customers in any new systems we might acquire or build," said Wilner. "The ESPN concept is unique and will be an attractive addition to our schedule."

ESPN will begin full-time, all-sports programming, via RCA's Satcom I, Transponder #7, beginning in September of 1979, highlighting a series of National Collegiate Athletic Association (NCAA) events in 18 sports.

"We are pleased that Vision Cable Communications has joined our growing list of affiliates," said Newman. "It is a very progressive company and its decision to carry ESPN programming shows foresight and confidence in sports programming on cable television."

-30-

CONTACT: DENNIS RANDALL (203) 747-6847

Vision Cable PR
COURTESY DENNIS RANDALL

Boxing and Canadian football. It set the stage for growth to the NHL, MLB, NBA, and NFL of today.

One last observation before a final sample of how we flooded the zone, not limited to our releases to editors. Cable and advertising lists got releases—no inbox digital missives. These were stamp licked stuffed envelopes, not the favorite final step to turning on the hose.

The Entertainment and Sports Programming Network Inc.

PRESENTS

NCAA SPORTS
The Championship Season

Football *Basketball*

Sampling of Games
from which ESPN will select
for 1979-80 distribution
to cable television systems throughout
the United States via RCA's Satcom I, Transponder #7.

NCAA original scheduling document
COURTESY DENNIS RANDALL

The Plainville dateline showed how much momentum got generated from the attic of 319 Cooke Street where doors on blocks served as early desks.

Was it exaggeration?

The Entertainment and Sports Programming Network Inc.
ESPN PLAZA ☐ BRISTOL, CONNECTICUT 06010 ☐ 203-584-8477

ESPN Will Televise
Davis Cup Zone Play

FOR IMMEDIATE RELEASE

PLAINVILLE, CT—The American Zone finals of the 1979 Davis Cup competition have been scheduled to be televised live by the Entertainment and Sports Programming Network, September 14, 15 and 16 from the Memphis (Tenn.) Tennis and Racquet Club.

Announcement of the telecast was made today by ESPN President Chester R. Simmons. Programming of the event is made available through the RCA Satcom I satellite, Transponder No. 7.

Argentina, Southern section winner, will oppose the United States squad, defending Davis Cup titlist and Northern sector finalist.

Guillermo Vilas, Jose Luis Clerc, Ricardo Cano and Player-Captain Lito Alvarez comprise the South American team. U.S. Captain Tony Trabert will announce his selections at a later date.

A pair of singles matches slated to begin at 5 p.m., Friday (14), a doubles match at 2:30 p.m., Saturday (15), and a windup of two singles matches to start at 2:30 p.m., Sunday (16) are featured in the best-of-five series. All times are EDT.

Last year's United States team subdued Great Britain in the Davis Cup finals, 4-1, behind singles players John McEnroe and Brian Gottfried and doubles representatives Stan Smith and Bob Lutz.

Two years ago, the U.S. was defeated by Argentina in the American Zone finals. The Argentineans, however, were ousted 3-2 in the 1978 American Zone semifinals by South American neighbor Chile.

The U.S. has encountered Argentina three times in Davis Cup competition and holds a 2-1 edge.

-30-

CONTACT: DENNIS RANDALL/MIKE CARUSO (203) 747-6847

ESPN PRESS-READY Davis Cup
COURTESY DENNIS RANDALL

Well, let's see, last I looked there was ESPN, ESPN2, ESPNW, ESPN Radio, and, yes as Ralph Voight quietly foretold in the analog explosion of all-sports television on September 9, 1979, there would be a digital revolution.

And, just like that, there was.

When Rosa Gatti was recruited by Chet Simmons to lead the PR efforts, she in turn recruited Chris LaPlaca, who as this is written is ESPN's senior vice president, corporate communications. He is responsible for the company's worldwide internal, public, and media relations strategies.

They would continue to flood the zone, Rosa retiring from ESPN in 2013. Chris offered his take on the 'SPNaut years:

I joined ESPN in July of 1980 as a communications assistant. I was one year out of college at St. Bonaventure.

What I remember most is a feeling of excitement and a can-do culture. We worked exceptionally hard . . . we had each other's backs . . . no job was too big or too small and it didn't matter what your job description was—if something needed to be done, and you were there, you did it.

My first day there I parked in front of the one building we had . . . which was right across the street from a scrap metal business. I was escorted through the broadcast center, out the back door, and ended up in a trailer. The place had already outgrown its physical space. I remember thinking: scrap metal . . . a folding table as a desk in a trailer . . . this is the future of sports television?

Chris LaPlaca 'SPNaut, former senior vice president for corporate communications, and longest-serving ESPN employee

COURTESY ESPN

Given my role in those very early days, pitching the promise of ESPN to media outlets all over the country, I remember a lot of doubters. It felt like nobody outside of ESPN thought this was a good idea, or an idea that could work . . . but WE did. We were sports fans serving other sports fans in ways not imagined before. And we all thought it was cool . . . so others would too . . . eventually!

I remember being in the broadcast center one weekend not long after I got there, because the cable guys had yet to come to my apartment and I wanted to watch what we were doing. We were doing a track meet from Rome, I believe, and I watched our tech crew bring the video through Australia and the audio through Japan and it ended up in Bristol at the same time and I thought that was just an unbelievable miracle. There weren't a lot of satellites in the sky at that time.

There was a wonderful mix of experience and youth. Some people left stable jobs at other networks or TV stations to take a chance. For me it wasn't a big risk. . . . I was a year out of college, not married, no kids, no mortgage. If it didn't work, so what? Rosa Gatti had come from Brown University and together we rolled up our sleeves. I will always be grateful she asked me to join her a week after she arrived.

Bill Rasmussen, our founder, was always around and always upbeat . . . his optimism and energy was infectious! Chet Simmons and Scotty Connal and Bill Fitts had done Super Bowls and Olympics and bowl games and World Series and they were the elders, bringing organization and focus that was desperately needed.

I remember driving Jim Simpson and Bud Wilkinson, two giants in broadcasting and coaching that I had watched on TV just a few years before, to a college football game in Athens, Georgia. They were there to broadcast the game. I was there to spread the word of ESPN, which most folks couldn't watch as cable was in its infancy. I couldn't believe that I, a young guy from a very small town, was now their colleague. None if it made sense but I faked it 'til I made it!

We didn't really have a business in the very early days, but we had passion and faith and each other. And it worked.

It is rare in anyone's life to be on the ground floor of something that would become so iconic and so ingrained in American culture. I feel so fortunate to have been among a small number of true pioneers.

CHAPTER 5

SportsCenter

THE PRICELESS FRANCHISE THAT IS *SPORTSCENTER* HAS BECOME ESPN's crown jewel.

While live sports now proliferate, there's only one *SportsCenter*. The incredible *SportsCenter* branded phenomenon separates ESPN from its current multitude of live sports competitors. Imitations are weak.

In the morass that has become televised live sports, ESPN's leadership continues with eight cable networks, a radio network, and direct-to-consumer and digital properties so numerous it takes fingers and toes to count. And they all get to leverage *SportsCenter*!

SportsCenter is sort of like a fleet of flagships, and its history is as old and as interesting as the sports behemoth itself.

If you dig deep and know the Rasmussen sports and broadcasting history, Bill will tell you about the half-hour sports news and highlights show he produced and delivered five nights a week on WHCT, a minor UHF signal in Hartford. He'll reminisce about the night on his program he had Hartford's boxing champ, Willie Pep, bring a few of his buddies to the studio for interviews. Imagine Bill's eyes when Rocky Graziano, Jake LaMotta, and Jersey Joe Walcott walked in.

Much has been written about the traffic jam that father and son Rasmussen endured on their way to daughter and sister Lynn's New Jersey shore birthday festivities. During the stall the satellite-driven awakening that seeded their dream took form, as did the strategy to go nationwide rather than statewide and leverage a willing relationship with UConn's athletic director to champion the concept inside the NCAA.

In his *Sports Junkies Rejoice,* Bill Rasmussen recounts the creation of *SportsCenter,* though it is nameless.

"More excited than ever, I suggested, let's get to the format. I think we can do four or five half-hour roundups a day and maybe 10 or 15 mini-updates in and around events."

At one point Bill is said to have begun calling it *SportsCentral.*

I was witness to the change to *SportsCenter.* Here's how that went:

When the Simmons/Connal NBC cavalry descended on our Plain-ville attic in the summer of 1979, they brought with them a familiar face in Jerry Moring.

Jerry came from WNBC Channel 4, in New York, but had spent a period in his career as news director of WHNB, the New Britain, Connecticut, NBC affiliate.

In conversation with Connal and Simmons I heard Jerry tell his bosses the name needed to be *SportsCenter,* not *SportsCentral.*

He built his argument on the use of *NewsCenter* by New York and Boston premier television news outlets, arguing that the nuance would be more readily accepted in large markets already using the *NewsCenter* promotional franchise.

SportsCenter it became, and if you notice in some of the early photography of the *SportsCenter* set, there's an obvious correcting overlay.

Harold Post, the local set builder who was executing the designs the NBC crew had drawn, was able to make the adjustment, and it became one of those *SportsCenter* trivia questions that's sure to win more than your usual bar bet.

In the true show business spirit, as neat and clean as the launch set looked that night, the surrounding chaos was epic. The late-summer sun hadn't set, and nobody told the bulldozer guys sculpting the backyard of the studio building. The audio guys went ballistic.

And not many knew the Total Sports Network that was going to bring viewers to sports heaven was being run from a couple of trailers and a rented remote truck hooked up to *SportsCenter.*

Early *SportsCenter* chaos stories abound and some may feel and read like *Clockwork Orange* delinquencies gone bad.

Take Bill Shanahan's streams of consciousness:

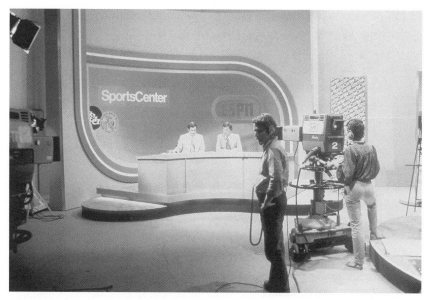

SportsCenter launch at 7:00 p.m., September 7, 1979. Anchors George Grande, left, and Lee Leonard; Bill Shanahan, floor manager, and Mary Walton on camera 2.
COURTESY BRISTOL HISTORICAL SOCIETY

I was the last of the original SportsCenter *crew to be hired, about a week before the network launched. Since the new building in Bristol was still under construction, ESPN was housed in the unfinished second floor of nearby United Cable.*

Six producer/directors and six production assistants comprised off camera SportsCenter. *Every day in the week leading up to the launch, the 12 of us would dutifully report to "the attic" to await instructions and directions to prepare this new studio show,* SportsCenter, *for its debut. And every day we would calmly wait for the expected intense brainstorming sessions with Jerry to begin. Every day. All around us in the one large attic room, those with other responsibilities were in a constant swirl of talking on telephones, huddling in twos and threes, examining documents on the various folding tables, etc.*

Our direct boss Jerry Moring, obviously harried and frustrated, occasionally would stop by his group to say something like, "sorry for the delay, we'll be meeting soon to review what we're going to do."

He would then rush on to whatever fire he had to put out, and we would continue to wait. Looking back, I now realize that each of us was privately thinking, "Man, I have no idea of what I'm expected to do, but I don't want to admit that out loud."

Gradually, as the group got to know each other and relaxed a bit, we began to develop a shared assessment of our situation. I believe the very first instance of the remarkable culture of humor that became a fundamental element of SportsCenter's success was when one of the group nicknamed our days in the attic "homeroom," serving little apparent purpose other than taking attendance and waiting to go to our first class.

After a few days, Jerry finally got us together to discuss what we'd be expected to do IN FOUR DAYS. We were going to produce a dual-anchor news show called SportsCenter, which would air twice a night and consist mainly of scores, game highlights, and news.

The shows would be 30 minutes long and would include commercial breaks. The producer/directors would have those roles for the shows, and the associate producers would be responsible for producing game highlights and other show elements.

That was it. Jerry had to rush off to yet another fire.

And as he was leaving, he mentioned we would do updates within whatever events ESPN was broadcasting between SportsCenter shows.

I remember us just sitting there for a bit, and I assume others were feeling much like I was, which was rising anxiety as to not having any idea where to even begin. It wasn't until a day later that one of the crew summoned up the nerve to ask out loud, "what's an update?"

Given the unstructured nature of homeroom week, and as an associate producer, I had no predetermined role on launch day. My general launch environment was of an energetic intensity that didn't quite get to actual panic, and I, like others from homeroom, just went with the flow of doing whatever task that seemed to be needed immediately.

I have this memory of there being no distinction between production people, technical people, or any other category. A sort of chaotic egalitarianism. I happened to hear that a taping in the studio needed a floor manager, so I just went to the studio to fill that need.

The taping turned out to be Lee Leonard's first words ever spoken on ESPN, "If you're a fan, IF you're a fan, you will think you have died and gone to sports heaven."

The responsibility for ESPN's welcoming launch sequence was with producers and a director from outside of SportsCenter. *The mounting pressure from the only-hours-to-air deadline to launch a first-of-its-type live national network became evident.*

Lee was seated on a generic office chair placed on a low riser against one wall of the studio. The studio lights and the intermittent air conditioning on a sunny early September day kept things toasty, and attractive to the several flies who wandered in to the doorless building.

As Lee sat patiently waiting to perform, the one or two camera operators silently waiting, I put on the floor manager's headset. In contrast to the silent studio, the headset was filled with several voices discussing what and how to do the taping. This went on for a while and steadily escalated into arguing that sometimes got quite strenuous and loud.

After a stretch of warm, quiet waiting, Lee calmly asks me, "may I ask why this is taking so long?" At that point the headset arguing was really loud and as I lifted it off my ear, the arguing could be heard across the silent studio. "Ah, I see," said Lee.

Looking back, Lee's veteran composure was just enough to offset the craziness around him and others.

Of course, the taping got done, as did the whole launch.

The studio ended up having a weird "eye of the hurricane" calmness so I didn't get swept into another fire drill. I ended up floor managing there for the rest of the launch.

The six producer/directors and six production assistants Bill Shanahan references are memorialized in the handwritten *SportsCenter* work schedules following the all-hands-on-deck launch weekend. These time capsule memories come from Shanahan musty boxes and represent producer/director and associate producer schedules for the first full week of *SportsCenter*'s existence.

From that associate producer cast, Bill and Tom Reilly went on to have long successful careers at ESPN, Reilly whose hijinks are as equally memorable as his talent. Reils proudly brought his own artifact out of mothballs.

In what became *SportsCenter*'s bread and butter, the highlight package, Tom's prior jack-of-all trades cable experience allowed him to collaborate with lead anchor George Grande to develop the staple shot

	MON. 10	TUES. 11	WED. 12	THURS. 13	FRI. 14	SAT. 15	SUN. 16
ANDY BRONSTEIN	10A-6P	10A-6P	10A-6P	OFF	OFF	4A-12P INSERTS + 9A PGM	4A-12P INSERTS + 9A PGM
PETER FOX	10A-6P	————	————	————	————>	OFF	OFF
CINDI MALYSZEK	12P-8P EDIT/TAPE NCAA-HILITES	OFF	OFF	10A-6P	10A-6P / 12P-8P	12P-8P INSERTS + 6P PGM	12P-8P INSERTS + 6P PGM
FRED MUZZY	8P-4A INSERTS			————>	OFF	OFF	8P-4A INSERTS
BOB PRONOVOST	2P 6P+11P PGMS				————>	OFF	OFF
DAVE SHEPPARD	12P-8P SCREEN&EDIT NCAA PREVUE	12P-8P TAPE NCAA PREVUE	OFF	OFF	8P-4A INSERTS	8P-4A INSERTS + 11P PGM	6P-?A ? PGM

Week One ESPN *SportsCenter* producer/director handwritten schedule
COURTESY BILL SHANAHAN

	MON. 10	TUES. 11	WED. 12	THURS. 13	FRI. 14	SAT. 15	SUN. 16
PAM BOUCHER	OFF	OFF	4P-12A	4P-12A	4P-12A	12P-8P BASEBALL	12P-8P BASEBALL
SARAH CHURCH	10A-6P	————	————	————>		OFF	OFF
CHRIS HOBIN	12P-8P	12P-8P	12P-8P	OFF	OFF	4A-12P	4A-12P
TOM REILLY	12P-8P EDIT/TAPE NCAA HILITES	OFF	OFF	4P-12A	4P-12A	12P-8P FOOTBALL	12P-8P FOOTBALL
BILL SHANAHAN	8P-4A	OFF	OFF	8P-4A	8P-4A	8P-4A	8P-4A
ELLIOT WARNER	4P-12A FOOTBALL	8P-4A BOB	8P-4A	OFF	OFF	12P-8P FOOTBALL	12P-8P FOOTBALL

Week One ESPN associate producer handwritten work schedule
COURTESY BILL SHANAHAN

sheet that for decades remained the life preserver of anchors, producers, and directors.

Tom Reilly tells the story of the shot sheet far better than I, so here is his version of its development and durability:

At the dawn of SportsCenter, *the mantra of our new bosses was: "It's all about the highlights."*

When you look at 40-plus years of SportsCenter *and how it's evolved, you realize just how prescient those words actually were. No show has ever done sports highlights better. In the beginning though, it was really a struggle.*

It was late August of 1979 and we were just two weeks away from the launch of ESPN. I was one of six original production assistants hired by SportsCenter *supervising producer, Jerry Moring. Jerry was one of many NBC Sports executives that jumped ship with Chet Simmons and Scotty Connal.*

He was vehement about getting the highlights right and then hoping that everything else would fall into place. Don't get me wrong, cutting sports highlights is not brain surgery. Many of the network sports divisions did a nice job with them at that time. However, they did not have to face the issues that our fledgling operation did.

We had so many, and some were glaring. The initial "friends and family" hiring spree was definitely a factor when it came to experience, and everyone needed to rally to the challenge.

George Grande was a class act. He had been hired to be one of the original anchors on SportsCenter. *George came from CBS Sports and was a pro in every sense of the word. Jerry told me to seek out George to get our highlight operation rolling. George had lots of experience with highlights.*

He was very positive, and immediately took me under his wing. He said the first step was to come up with our version of a "shot sheet" which I had some experience with as well. We talked about the "situation," the "action," and the "result" blocks.

He told me to come up with a template that had those three-column blocks with the widest being the "action" block. I came back with one that had five shots per page, with a game title and date header. Pretty basic, but "voila!" the SportsCenter *shot sheet was born. It's the same template that's used today inside the screening computers 40 years later!*

As an example, here's what the shot sheet I wrote might have looked like for Game 7 of the World Series that year:

Perhaps the biggest challenge of all in those fateful early days was that we were a highlight show that couldn't show highlights! It wasn't pretty.

None of the networks would let us show same-day highlights of any professional sports!

We had no major professional sports rights or reciprocity like the major networks shared with each other, so technically we could only show NCAA sports highlights or the minor sports to which we had the rights. Case in point, the very first highlights we ever showed on SportsCenter, were UConn vs. Indiana soccer, and the American Professional Slow Pitch Softball Championship between the Kentucky Bourbons and the Milwaukee Schlitz.

MLB took a particularly hard line that we were not a news show. They argued that because we were a highlight show, we could not use highlights under "the NEWS guise" like network affiliates during their news shows.

WORLD SERIES GAME 7		10/17/79
SITUATION	ACTION	RESULT
MEMORIAL STADIUM IN BALTIMORE BOTTOM 3rd SCORELESS	JIM BIBBY DELIVERS A FASTBALL TO RICH DAUER WHO LINES IT DEEP TO LEFT INTO THE SEATS	1 - 0 ORIOLES CROWD IN A FRENZY
TOP 6th STILL 1 - 0	WILLIE STARGELL CRUSHES THIS SCOTT McGREGOR FASTBALL DEEP TO RIGHT FIELD AND GONE! BILL ROBINSON ABOARD...	2 - 1 PIRATES BENCH EXPLODES
TOP 9th	OMAR MORENO RIPS A SINGLE UP THE MIDDLE OFF MIKE FLANAGAN SCORING PHIL GARNER WITH THE INSURANCE RUN	3 - 1 PIRATES
BOTTOM 9th 4 - 1 PIRATES	KENT TEKULVE GETS PINCH HITTER PAT KELLY TO FLY TO RIGHT CENTER... OMAR MORENO SQUEEZES IT!	PIRATES WIN THE WORLD SERIES 4 GAMES TO 3!
	WILD CELEBRATION PIRATES MOB MVP WILLIE STARGELL CUE UP "WE ARE FAMILY"	

ORIGINAL ESPN HIGHLIGHTS TEMPLATE RE-CREATED BY TOM REILLY

Looking back it's hard to believe that we were only allowed to show the previous day's highlights after we showed that day's scores! It was just awful. It was basically yesterday's news today. Our legal department was in full battle mode.

The edict soon came down for our anchors to stress that we were a comprehensive sports NEWS show. It wasn't hard to prove because without professional sports highlights we did "reader" after "reader" of on-camera sports news. It became a major concern for our credibility.

Finally, just before the MLB playoffs started, our president, Chet Simmons said, "Fuck it, we're showing highlights! Let 'em sue us!" (or something close to that).

We were all ecstatic, but we still had to limit ourselves as if we were a local newscast. We could only show two minutes of MLB highlights in a given half-hour show. Gradually, we got bolder and bolder with our usage. We kept our legal department very busy.

Negotiations were contentious, particularly with baseball. We would get updates it seemed like every week. If we wanted to use MLB footage that was more than 24 hours old for news stories, interviews, or features, it cost us $10 a second. The NFL was just as bad and quickly followed suit. The NBA and NHL were not quite as tough, but pretty similar with their restrictions.

It seemed like all the professional sports leagues wanted us to fail. They made it very challenging for our new SportsCenter staff and our fledgling sports highlights show . . . Excuse me, sports NEWS show!

It was now the first week of October, and the Pirates had just beaten the Reds in the 1979 NLCS. I was editing the highlight of the game dominated by series MVP Willie Stargell.

My producer Bobby Pronovost told me I could go a minute in length, so I was psyched! Imagine that, a full minute! The edit bay was still in a trailer outside of our unfinished broadcast center. As I was telling our editor Jerry Weed what the next shot was, the door opened behind us and up the stairs popped a very tall dark figure.

I looked behind me in the dim light as a long arm reached out to shake my hand . . . "Hi, how ya doin,' Chris Berman . . . mind if I watch?" After introductions we started to talk about how amazing "Pops" Stargell was, and what I had planned for the highlight. We hit it off immediately.

Right away I could see his tremendous passion for sports and television. I could sense his excitement for what we were both getting into at ESPN. Little did I know just how iconic my new coworker would become.

Little did I know he was "all about the highlights" and no one would ever do them better.
Little did I know that he would become one of my best friends in life.

The professional rigors of launching ESPN, *SportsCenter*, and revolutionizing sports television take no back seat to the personal rigors: for instance the heralded Fly Break during program prep, as remembered with shivers by many. The late-summer humidity and wide-open building under construction invited *Musca domestica Linnaeus* to sup on crumbs left aside *SportsCenter*'s newsroom folding tables. We'd hunch over assignments, buzzed in ways we didn't choose, and irritated by the damned flies until one of us would call for a Fly Break!

Instantly, we'd lurch for a folded newspaper and the great newsroom swat would begin, unrelenting, angry swatting, until energy drained, and flies dead, we'd return to assignments.

It wasn't the only wildlife-related exasperating issue the open-air building begat.

The *SportsCenter* studio had its real life Pepé Le Pew, and while an actual sighting is shrouded in rumor, it's seemingly everlasting and certainly breathtaking residue left unmistakable evidence of its visits.

Pepé was mostly nocturnal, though his leave-behinds lingered. Boomer Berman was nocturnal, too, specializing early on in the late-night West Coast edition of *SportsCenter*. About Pepé, Boomer says: "Did I see him? No. Did I know he was there for two weeks? You betcha." When asked if anybody saw Pepé, he thought Chuck Pagano may have. And in Berman's inimitable way he 180'd the conversation saying, "did you know it was Chuck who nicknamed me Boomer?"

Chris continued admitting he wasn't spot on with the nickname quote, but remembered strolling into the control room after signing off with a strong highlight package to hear Chuck say something like: "You really blew those out, Chris. We should just call you the boomer."

And it stuck. Boy, did it.

The *SportsCenter* team surely wears the 'SPNaut tattoo with an asterisk for creativity, and guts. The names that didn't make it to this printed launch highlight reel such as Andy Bronstein, Elliot Warner, Cindy

Malyszek, Chris Hobin, and Sarah Church earn everlasting kudos for grinding through the demanding early days.

SportsCenter history dares not be ended without the memory of one Fred Muzzy, a talent, a clown, a man with a heart the size of his waist. Fred Muzzy is legendary for his outlandish remarks, and perhaps an unplanned mishap that demands retelling.

It's a you-had-to-be-there moment. The telling requires a setup; maybe even this picture sells what happened.

What the photo won't show is the torrential rain that filled a waist-deep hole between the administration trailer and the main door to the unfinished building.

Fred thought it was just a puddle. He didn't drown, but our laughter drowned his cavalier presence as he strolled into the downstairs temporary news area looking like a soaked doughboy, and insisted on working up the next *SportsCenter* stories board.

In Chapter 7 we'll visit ESPN's ladies of the night, 'SPNauts all, but any effort to speak to the original *SportsCenter* would be incomplete without full mention of the first woman *SportsCenter* anchor, **Rhonda Glenn.** It didn't take long for Rhonda, joining *SportsCenter* and carving a historic niche for herself as the first national network woman sportscaster.

ESPN SportsCenter
Under Construction
Summer 1979

ESPN construction
PHOTO COURTESY BILL RASMUSSEN

Rhonda's standout golfing career attested to her sports acumen, and her television skills were honed as a sports reporter in Norfolk, Virginia, and as a part-time golf analyst with ABC.

Her love of golf took her to an eventual communications position with the United States Golf Association, but not before leaving a strong mark as *SportsCenter*'s Sally Ride, befitting her surname and the 'SPNaut wings she sports.

Dave Sheppard filled out the Scotty Connal producer/director hirings, and like a lot of us, got toasted by the young man's world of live television. When we reconnected, Dave spoke of his family and his 180 professional turnabout. When he returned to Bristol on the occasion of ESPN's 40th Anniversary celebration, he smiled when after renewing friendships and attendant good feelings his wife said to him, "You didn't tell me you were such a big thing."

We didn't know then. We do now. Here's Dave's essay on those early times:

Rhonda Glenn, first woman sports network anchor
COURTESY ESPN

In the summer of 1979 I was working at Connecticut Public Television in Hartford on the production crew.

Word started spreading around that there was this new cable network coming to the area called ESPN. Cable networks were in their infancy then, and nobody had any real idea of what they were, or what they were trying to do. We heard that this would be an all-sports network, and they were hiring! At public television we cover everything, so I had some background in televised sports, though I didn't consider myself to be a "sports guy." However I was, most definitely, a "TV guy," and was looking to take the next step on my career path. So I sent in my resume hoping that just maybe someone would see it.

A couple of weeks later I got a response. They wanted to interview me! Holy ____! I managed to find a jacket and tie, and went to the temporary home of ESPN at the local cable company office. I was asked to wait in the conference room, and sat at a table that must have had several hundred resumes just in piles. Of course I peeked at them, and was amazed. There were people applying who had years of network sports experience, and here I was a kid from the local PBS station who wanted to be a director. I figured I didn't have a chance, but what the hell, I was already there.

Several minutes later this tall guy comes in who looks like he had been running in 10 directions at once. He apologized for the delay and introduced himself; Scotty Connal. Truth be told, I had no idea of who he was. I just knew this would be my only shot at getting hired. He explained what ESPN was about, and what he was hoping it would be, then asked why he should hire me. I said something like I knew I was young and didn't have the depth of experience he might be looking for, but I was willing to do anything he needed, and work my butt off doing it. Apparently that made an impression because he told me he appreciated the honesty, and hired me on the spot. He told me the salary, I agreed, we shook hands, and that was it.

About two weeks later, Tuesday September 4, 1979, was my first day. I remember we met in what would become the first newsroom at ESPN. Nobody knew anyone else, so it was a jumble of introductions and comparing backgrounds. Finally in comes Jerry Moring, the executive producer of studio shows. He explained that he had been in that same role at the NBC station in New York City, and had named the local newscast NewsCenter 4. He thought it would be a good thing to call our news department SportsCenter, and so the anchor of the network was born. There were six of us as producer/directors, and another six as assistant p/d's, and we would be doing everything that came out of the studio; newscasts, weekly football, basketball, hockey, or whatever wrap-ups, and anything else that came along.

Come Friday night, September 7, 1979, 7 p.m., and ESPN was live. I found myself in the remote truck that was our control room coordinating the first sporting event ever shown, The slow-pitch softball World Series. The video quality was terrible as it was a night game with very little lighting, but we were on the air, and ESPN was a reality.

Randomly I was assigned the weekly NCAA football show hosted by broadcasting legend Jim Simpson and College Football Hall of Famer Bud Wilkinson. These two titans of their respective industries had to put up with me, and us, making everything up as we went along. Many times they took the bits and pieces we managed to pull together, and with their combined experience, created an intelligent and informative show.

Since the football show went so well, or at least wasn't bad, when the college basketball season rolled around we took the same format but this time with Bob Ley hosting with this guy named Dick Vitale. I had no idea who Dick was, but it soon became very apparent that he was lightning in a bottle. Bob had the Herculean task of trying to keep Dick under control on the air,

Dave Sheppard standing, Bud Wilkinson and Jim Simpson seated
COURTESY DAVE SHEPPARD

and mostly was successful, but you never knew what he might say. That was part of Dick's appeal; he was the ultimate straight-shooter.

Our final regular show of the season was to cover the selection of teams to go to the NCAA tournament, "March Madness." These were always live announcements, and we had to be ready to show highlights of the teams and matchups of who was playing who. Well 32 teams would be announced, but we wouldn't know them until it happened. Luckily, somehow, Jules Winn from the programming department was able to get word of the teams about 15 minutes before we went on the air. It was total chaos and adrenaline from that point on. We had prepared highlights packages and graphics for about 100 teams so now we had to get it organized. Somehow it worked. All I remember is that there were 3/4-inch videotape cassettes being thrown across the room, matchup brackets being typed up seconds before being put on the air, me directing it all and trying not to have my head explode, and Bob giving his usual silken delivery of all this information. The 30-minute show felt like it happened in 15 seconds, but we had done it. No network had ever covered the selection announcement live before. We had just made TV history.

The last piece of the basketball season puzzle is always the "Final Four," which is championship weekend. So off to Indianapolis we go: myself, Bob Ley, and cameraman extraordinaire Jeff Israel. We did interviews in and around the two semifinal games on Saturday, more on Sunday, and were in the stands watching the final on Monday. With about five minutes to go Bob says, "c'mon, let's get ready for the postgame and get down to courtside." At the final buzzer we were part of the tsunami of reporters flooding the court to get interviews. Now remember, this was before wireless mics so the three of us were tethered together with various cables. Somehow Bob got the interviews, Jeff got the shots, and I was taking notes and shooting stills. We didn't have any way to transmit back to ESPN, so it was an early flight the next day to the studio so we could edit packages together, and go live that evening. By today's standards, it's the equivalent of cave drawings, but it's what we had, so we made it work. I remember Scotty coming up to us when we got back to say how proud he was to see us storming the court in our red-and-white ESPN jackets.

I was lucky enough to be part of so many "firsts" at ESPN. Two weeks after the NCAA championship I was directing the studio side of the first-ever NFL draft coverage, again something that had never been done. One day in the newsroom Scotty came running in to tell us that somehow we had the rights to the soccer World Cup, and we had to get on the air immediately. This *was, after all, probably the world's largest sporting event and we had it. Who knew! Again, somehow, we pulled together a studio show with live coverage of the games. The following summer I was in the back of a 40-foot boat trying not to be seasick while covering the America's Cup races in Newport, Rhode Island. It was events like these that formed the foundation and framework of what ESPN would become. In those first days, weeks, and months what made it all possible was a mutual love of what we were doing. There weren't any rules, no previous formats to follow, and very few restrictions. We all did whatever we had to do to put these shows together and get them on the air. Soon enough the free for all had to be tamed; this was a business after all and a whole lot of money was on the line. People and productions had to be accountable, and honestly, the fun part died a little.*

I left after about three years, and the growth has been beyond anything I ever imagined. I went back to Bristol for the 40th anniversary and was astounded at what ESPN is today. The first studio is still there, and the control room is now an office. When I walked into those rooms the memories came flooding back. At the end of every NCAA Basketball Tournament they play the song "One Shining Moment" to a montage of highlights. That's what the first days of ESPN will always be to me; a series of shining moments that I'll never forget.

SportsCenter became the model, often imitated, etc. etc. I rather think of the ESPN flagship *SportsCenter* in the terms Mae West accorded herself: "I'm no model. A model's just an imitation of the real thing," she scolded.

True *SportsCenter* builders know who they are. Those iconic early faces and voices set a tone that gave sports fans everywhere a go-to sports authority in an immediate, sometimes intimate and reliably informative program.

The original *SportsCenter* triple threat iconics are a pair of recognizable talents and a ghost, supported by a pride of other young lions.

CHAPTER 6

Two Famous Faces, a Ghost, and a Posse

TWO EARLY 'SPNAUT ON-AIR PERSONALITIES BECAME FAMOUS AND familiar over decades; a third continues to haunt the ESPN family because the bright candle of Tom Mees's exceptional 'SPNaut talent was extinguished in a still-unexplained drowning accident.

Chris "Boomer" Berman and I continue to enjoy a relationship which grew closer as we dilly-dallied in golf circles after Simmons and Connal finally cleansed ESPN of the daily talents of Bill Rasmussen and me.

Tom Mees, Chris Berman, and Bob Ley
PHOTO COURTESY THE RICK LA BRANCHE ESTATE

Bob Ley, always the gentleman, walked into *SportsCenter* on the weekend of launch and introduced himself to me and his peers, sat down, rolled up his sleeves and began a career that to his everlasting credit turned a new leaf for sports journalism past rip-and-read score reporting. It's best told by Bob himself:

It was the phone call that would change my life, and it woke me out of a deep sleep. It was past 9 a.m. on a Monday in August 1979, and I want to remember that we had been working hard the night before at the local cable station where I was sports director. But it's entirely possible that both our usual maniacal labor and a bit of youthful decompression had contributed to my somnambulant state.

By the time I staggered to the phone on the wall of the kitchen in the large apartment I shared with two coworkers, I was almost coherent. And about 15 seconds into the phone call, I realized that the letter and resume tape I had dispatched several weeks ago had at least provoked an inquiry. Somehow I located a pen and a paper and scratched out some details, an address, some rudimentary directions, and engaged in a conversation with a pleasant voice on the other end of the phone.

We had a date to meet Friday, four days hence, about 100 miles away in Plainville, Connecticut. But wait. The early moments of this call had been a fuzzy memory.

"I'm sorry, I didn't get your name," I ventured.

"It's Scotty Connal," came the response.

Now I was fully, transcendently awake. We hung up. And I took a breath.

This was the big leagues. He was big-league. Everyone knew Scotty Connal, the former executive producer of NBC Sports. In charge of all the shows and sports. The guy who, four years earlier, had innovatively placed a camera inside Fenway Park's Green Monster scoreboard for the World Series. That simply produced one of the epic images of the 20th century: Carlton Fisk waving his historic Game 6 home run fair.

He was the executive who wanted to talk to me about a job at this new entity, ESPN.

But it wouldn't be that simple.

I drove into work that day, and within 90 minutes the phone rang with another potential pivot point in my career. It was New Jersey Public

Television's news director wanting to talk to me about their #2 sports position. We had a date to talk Saturday, five miles away, in Newark.

I knew I was in a fortunate position, but at the age of 24, hauling down an impressive $13K a year (plus the lofty $100 per game I made as public address announcer for soccer's fabled Cosmos), I didn't fully appreciate how lucky I was.

So that on the appointed Friday, after meeting with Scotty and newsroom chief Jerry Moring, I was being walked to the door by Scotty. It was exactly two weeks before ESPN's sign-on. The unfinished second floor of the United Cable building in Plainville was a landscape of energy and activity. Only in hindsight can I appreciate what these people were trying to pull off, fully committed to a sign-on date, and trying to staff up a "network" virtually from scratch. If they were nervous—and they certainly were—they weren't showing that to this kid from Jersey.

Somewhere in the conversation with Scotty, I had been offered a job, at virtually double my current salary. Who wouldn't jump at that?

"One thing, Mr. Connal," I explained as we got to the door. "I do have another job interview tomorrow. So I'll have to get back to you."

He stopped in his tracks. I want to remember that he took this in stride. I can only imagine what was flying through his mind and his stomach.

I promised Scotty an answer by the end of the weekend.

The next day produced another job offer, at virtually identical money, with the enticing prospect of anchoring weekend sports in New York and Philadelphia on the NJPTV network. That, plus covering major-league teams and reporting through the week.

I had 18 hours to make up my mind. And it looked like an easy call.

Take the position that would not require me to relocate. The job which would put me on the air in the #1 and #4 markets, with a world of possibilities. After all, that operation in Connecticut was literally working out of trailers, still constructing the studio, with Port-o-sans and food trucks sustaining the effort.

But I was departing my job in local cable at a station, TV3 Suburban Cablevision, where I had been hired three years earlier, shaking hands on the deal over the literal blueprints of a remote van that was still being built. And over the ensuing months and years, I had seen firsthand what the freedom and opportunity of a startup meant.

Sunday, I picked up the phone and told Scotty I was signing on. He was ebullient.

Just as when I walked into the Bristol facility on Sunday, September 9, deep into ESPN's first weekend on the air. My car was in the unpaved parking lot, filled with my stuff. I found the one working master control room, crowded with anxious and hopeful faces, empty pizza boxes and soda cans. Scotty spied me.

"See? Lookit!" he beamed, pointing at the wall of monitors showing our programming. "We're on the air!"

Indeed we were. A hardy band of pioneers bound by opportunity and now, necessity. Lifetime friendships would take root. Careers and legends would be created. But right now, we were on the air. And there was no signing off.

People who mourn Tom Mees have unique personal memories of him. He had a unique talent that was immediately recognized by those of us who viewed his audition tape.

In the warm summer United Cable attic where Scotty Connal was interviewing, hiring and auditioning talent, I remember when he called out to those of us supporting his search, to "come look at this."

He was viewing Tom Mees's audition tape and observed that in the several minutes that Mees provided he did not mispronounce a syllable. Connal wanted Mees on the team for his exceptional presentation.

Tom went on to read a gazillion sports highlight reels live and impeccably during the hundreds of *SportsCenter* airings he anchored.

Chris remembered his friend and teammate this way: "Tom had a sense of purity in the way he loved sports and it showed in the spirit that was so obvious on TV and off."

I met Chris Berman months before the NBC cavalry galloped up the East Side Highway and Merritt Parkway to set up camp with us in the United Cable attic.

Lou Palmer and I occupied the first two desks in that attic and one late morning we got a heads-up from Vivian Arsego, who was backing up Bill, Scott, Ed, and Bob in our tiny downstairs space and acting as our gatekeeper.

She told us there was a big guy down there who wanted to apply for an announcer's job.

As is Lou's way, he waved Chris up to our lair, but I was late-morning jittery and cooked up a reason about worrying outsiders believing a network was being hatched in an attic, so suggested lunch.

Off we went, I recall distinctly, to the lounge at the Corner House restaurant where lunch was great and I knew the barkeep would slip me another whatever on the house while Lou, Chris, and I talked sports TV.

Chris's presence, even then, was not overwhelming but big, like his football and first baseman's stature would attest. Professionally attracted to Chris, I fibbed that even Lou and I were working on the cuff, to get ESPN started, because I felt bad, two libations into the conversation, that I'd have to turn down Chris.

The to-be-Boomer didn't flinch. In fact, Chris told me he would keep knocking on ESPN's door until we did hire him.

What even Chris, Lou, and I didn't know at the time was that Chris was hoping he would get his shot when the Scotty entourage arrived and it became clear that Connal was doing the talent hiring.

In a story that Chris told me he'd never revealed, he actually had a relationship with Scotty Connal that went back to Chris's college years. He tells it this way:

While I was at Brown, my parents said they had a friend, Julian Goodman, who knew some big wheels at NBC Sports on my behalf. Well Julian connected with Scotty Connal who agreed to have a chat with me.

It really was a chat, it didn't feel like an interview, and we spoke about broadcasting philosophically, Scotty advising that announcing was like being a chef, on-air style being a blend of styles absorbed and created.

Scotty slipped in NBC's fall broadcasting of American Football League games and that he might need someone to babysit the open phone line between production trucks and NBC headquarters, during New England Patriots home games.

"How would that sound to you," Scotty asked. And I couldn't believe he was offering the opportunity at $50 a game, nothing for a college kid to laugh at in 1975.

Chris's NBC stints expanded when the Red Sox won the American League pennant and competed against Cincinnati's Big Red Machine in

1975, in Curt Gowdy's broadcast booth as an as-needed runner for the crew around Fenway Park.

Three years later as Chris interviewed formally at ESPN, he remembers saying to Connal that he wasn't sure Scotty remembered him, and was assured that he did.

"He offered me the late-night *SportsCenter* anchor job, saying because I spoke in complete sentences and the NBC guys in the truck liked me."

Chris Berman is hard not to like. In other ways we continued to work together outside of ESPN and a friendship bloomed.

In another life, a sober one, I'd migrated to Naples, Florida, where at the time there were more golf holes per capita than anywhere else in the country.

Once again Bill Rasmussen put out a call for help, and I responded to his need for a promotion leader in the PGA Senior Tour event his new company, Intellinet, had agreed to sponsor. It was fun to saddle up with Bill again.

We innovated, even straining the tour's protocols and leveraging our friendships with ESPN covering crews to add time to their broadcast to cover the Golf Sprint we concocted.

The Intellinet Golf Sprint teamed 18 of Naples's best golfers, nine men and nine women, who golfed one ball around the 18-hole layout in 14 minutes and 38 seconds.

After the tourney I met a man in Naples, Larry Olsen of Chicago, who had just taken control of a golf company, Natural Golf, which needed a communications expert: I convinced him that person was me.

In another whirlwind startup frenzy, I convinced Chris Berman, not only to become a Natural Golfer, but a Natural Golf endorser and even stockholder.

Chris and I remembered the freezing day we met to introduce him to Natural Golf's single-plane golf swing modeled after Canadian golf savant Moe Norman. At the invitation of Chet Dunlop, himself a pioneering golf instructor, Chris and I met at the driving net in the large barn Chet heated for us in his freshly accommodating way. I taught an enthusiastic Chris the Moe Norman way there and later at his vacation spot on Sanibel Island.

Natural Golfer magazine

Peter Fox and Chris Berman at Sanibel Island

A season later, I walked inside the ropes with Chris and his PGA Touring friend Joey Sindelar at the Travelers Pro Am where Chris went out and shot a high handicapped 39 on the front nine, prompting Sindelar to ask me, "What have you taught my partner?"

We shared the Moe Norman–inspired euphoria until the back nine. He still carries a Natural Golf 5 wood, and we both shrugged off its bankruptcy.

We didn't shrug off a friendship, and Chris particularly wanted to be part of the documentary we worked on commemorating Moe Norman's golfing genius.

Bob Ley and Chris remained at ESPN through Ralph Voight's prescient transition from analog to digital revolution, Y2K, and the sunrise of streaming video that threatens to kill cable but not the concept that sports fans have an appetite for watching sports any way you feed them.

Bob Ley, Chris Berman, and the late Tom Mees are not the only 'SPNauts admired for the faith, energy, and even a smidgeon of naïveté that led sports fans to a new way to get sports news.

Early pros like Lee Leonard, George Grande, Bob Waller, and of course Lou Palmer and Greg Wyatt deserve credit as ESPN birthing accoucheurs.

The late Lee Leonard and Bob Waller had stints at CNN, Lou and George to their baseball first loves, Lou with the Marlins, George in the Yankees and Reds broadcast booths.

Greg recalled being tracked down in a tiny Baja village with one phone, a pure hideaway he and his wife were enjoying. On the horn was Scotty Connal, who was convinced that Greg's feature work at NBC Sports would translate at *SportsCenter*.

In Greg's own words:

> *I was on cloud nine when we started ESPN. I had worked for Scotty and Chet at NBC Sports but never met them until our meeting in the attic at United Cable the week before ESPN signed on. Now I look back 40 years later and realize what was accomplished by you, Bill Rasmussen, his son Scott, and Lou Palmer was historic in broadcasting. I am so proud to be a '79er.*

Greg Wyatt 'SPNaut '79
COURTESY G. WYATT

Supporting the famous 'SPNaut faces are behind-the-scenes producers, directors, and assistants, some infamous, who joined in the last trimester and infancy of the satellite-inseminated cable television revolution.

One of the swashbucklers was a sassy youngster, **Tom Reilly**, who went on to become a strong cog in the ESPN machine. Reilly hired as an associate producer, was another of the Connecticut gold coast trickle-down invites by Scotty Connal.

The Reilly ESPN hiring story has a familiar ring, though special nuance.

Reilly teases it as "Cryptic words from my future boss." This is how it goes:

It was July of 1979. I was living in Greenwich, Connecticut, and luckily, so was Scotty Connal, VP of operations for NBC Sports.

I was working three jobs at the time: painting houses, bartending at Augie's, and commuting part-time to UA Columbia Cable TV in Pompton Lakes, New Jersey.

I knew that sports television was what I wanted to pursue in life. After a heartbreakingly close call at an entry-level job with ABC Sports, I was more determined than ever. I knew a lot of people in town who knew Scotty Connal and I pestered his office with phone calls for months. Persistence paid off and I finally got my interview at "30 Rock."

After shaking hands, he sat down at his impressive desk and said, "So what's your story Reilly?" I told him that I had majored in Visual Studies and Architecture at Dartmouth, but I always wanted to get into sports. I told him the story of how I met Frank Gifford, my childhood idol who happened to be playing tennis with the owner of the house I was painting, who was a friend of the family.

They invited me to join them for a cocktail and Frank ultimately got my foot in the door at ABC Sports. I was a finalist for four production assistant positions with more than 100 applicants. I was interviewed three times by network heavyweights Chet Forte, Dennis Lewin, and John Martin.

Predictably I just missed out on the job because I didn't have any TV production experience. I then told Scotty that I solved that problem by going to UA Columbia Cable and lying to them about being an undergraduate intern.

After a few months I was hands-on indispensable in their local cable sports productions; shooting, editing, reporting, and calling games. I finally fessed up and they hired me.

Scotty loved that story and proceeded to ask me what I thought I could contribute to NBC Sports. Just as I began to tell him how well I could cut highlights, his secretary buzzed him about a very important call. "Sorry Tom I really have to take this call right now, so just go back into the waiting room and make yourself comfortable for a few minutes."

After what seemed like forever, he finally summoned me back in and said something I will never forget: "Sorry about the wait Tom but that was a very interesting phone call. In fact, it was about something that would really interest you as well."

I just stared at him. Was I really hearing these cryptic words from an iconic television executive that I hardly knew? He was smiling. I continued to stare at him incredulously. I was looking for an explanation, but he said, "That's all I can tell you right now Tom, but it is something that could be part of your future."

At this point I didn't really know how to react. I was so confused. Was he talking about NBC Sports? The interview ended fairly quickly. He told me he had heard enough and would call me back in a few weeks.

I walked out of his office completely mystified, but I was excited beyond belief! What the hell was that phone call all about? I could hardly contain myself!

I left for LA the next day to visit my twin sister, and for three more job interviews. Two weeks later I had a job offer from TWI Productions to do interviews and help cut features previewing the 1980 Summer Olympics in Moscow (we hadn't boycotted them yet). It had been a great trip and things seemed to be going my way.

Then it happened.

On the plane ride home, I opened the LA Times *sports section to the headline: "NBC Sports Executives to Run 24-Hour Sports Network, ESPN." I broke out into a huge grin and hooted as I read the details! NBC Sports president Chet Simmons and vice president Scotty Connal were jumping ship and taking a leap of faith to run a 24-hour cable sports network: wow!*

Now I knew what that phone call was about! The mystery was solved! I was so pumped up I couldn't wait to call Scotty the next day.

I remember when he answered the phone he laughed and said, "I told you you'd be interested! When can you start?" I couldn't believe my ears and I blurted out, "anytime! I'll be there tomorrow if you need me to be!" He chuckled, "well that's great but two weeks would probably be best because the building, control room, and studio are not even finished yet." That was the understatement of all time as we would soon find out.

"A guy named Jerry Moring will call you tomorrow with all the details. I hope you're ready to work your balls off because that's what it's going to take to pull this thing off. Congratulations and I'll see you up in Bristol ."

Talk about fate. . . . It's still hard to fathom that the phone call which finalized Scotty Connal's decision to change the course of sports television happened in the middle of my interview! The timing and odds of that happening have made me smile many times throughout my career.

Jerry Moring did call the next day and officially hired me as one of six original production assistants for a new show called SportsCenter. *He said it would be ESPN's flagship studio show for highlights, scores, interviews, and news, but he emphasized that the biggest thing was the highlights.*

"We need to figure out the highlights! Scotty thinks you're up to the task. I hope he's right, because honestly, we don't have a lot of people who have really done that. If you do that, and help the group get up to speed, we'll bump you to associate producer in no time."

I was so excited my mind was racing at Mach speed. I knew they had found the right guy and that big things were about to happen. I just didn't know how tough it was going to be getting there.

The first few weeks and months were truly unbelievable. The obstacles we all overcame were just mind boggling. It was pretty scary at times, but boy was it ever fun!

Another 'SPNaut and Connal Cavalry soldier is **Jim Rosenberg**. Jim was a strong utility player in the television production arena who brought a reliable steadiness to whatever was thrown his way.

Virtually alone he managed ESPN's early commitment to Professional Bowling programs. Jim's soldiering went well beyond what he brought to ESPN. Just recently he was allowed to share his real soldiering, when he and his peers were finally publicly recognized for their unique service in support of nuclear deterrence. Before his ESPN years, he had been involved in testing nuclear weapons as part of the secretive Operation Castle on the Eniwetak atoll in the Marshall Islands.

It's hard not to write about ESPN early on-air personalities without mention of the mouth that soars, **Dick Vitale**.

Dick Vitale called his first game with ESPN on December 5, 1979, shortly after the company's September 7 launch. ESPN archivists remembered his 40 years on the call of college basketball this way:

"Forty years later, Vitale is a college basketball icon, whose mere presence in an arena signifies a game's magnitude and sends fans into a frenzy. Through it all, Vitale has always remembered his roots and has become a passionate fundraiser in the fight to end cancer."

"Forty years! It blows my mind," Vitale said. "I remember walking in doing that first game, and it seems like yesterday. I can't believe how 40 years have just flown by. It's been a journey that's exceeded any dream I ever had. I owe so much of my career to all the beautiful people at ESPN and the incredible college basketball fans."

'SPNaut Dick Vitale
COURTESY ESPN

As this is being written Dick Vitale is recovering from a second bout with throat cancer and was understandably unavailable for an interview, though his soaring "diaper dandies" and "gimme the rock" are unforgettable basketball lexicon treasures.

CHAPTER 7

Ladies of the Night

IN WHAT WAS A TESTOSTERONE-FLOODED POPULATION OF 'ESPNAUTS, the studio crew that nightly delivered *SportsCenter* was estrogenically strong too.

Three women immediately come to mind.

Mary Walton is a special friend, a special talent, a special woman, and an 'SPNaut of the highest order. That's Mary on the cover of this book.

We met earlier in the 1970s while I was romancing her knockout pool-sharking pal, Lynn Bermingham. I introduced Mary to a colleague and an equally fast romance ensued that brought us together often.

Mary, then a contract photographer for the *Hartford Courant*, was bold and ambitious with amazing chops and defied my only effort at mentoring:

Mary announced one day she was going to produce and act in an amateur theater production of *Hot L Baltimore* to add to her artistic curriculum vitae.

"Too much," I advised. "You'll be better off doing one well than two roles halfway," I expect were close to the words I used.

Of course, she was great at both and the play was a hit, and even seemed to have a role for a character, Mr. Morse, a wine-odorous Hot L Baltimore lobby fixture in which the producer cast yours truly.

Mr. Morse lay about the lobby for most of the three acts, only startled awake once in a while by catfighting hookers. Here's a Mr. Morse shot Mary took during dress rehearsals.

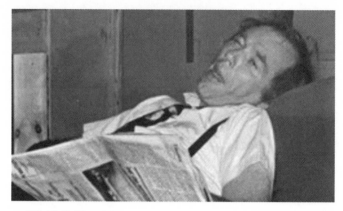

Mr. Morse of Hot L Baltimore
COURTESY OF MARY WALTON

While 'SPNauts arrived in 1978, 1979, and even 1980 in earned cases, Mary Walton joins the very select group who staged the first-ever telecast, the aforementioned November 17, 1978 production of UConn basketball.

Mary was assigned to shoot still photos for Dennis Randall's PR use. In my mind I still can see the holy grail shot she took of us walking out of the Telfax truck with a pair of hour-long canisters of two-inch video-tape, one in each hand after the thrilling premiere. It, too, is in the ether.

Mary became an early fixture in the ESPN studio, on camera. Her recollections here were prefaced with a disclaimer that her memories today are scant, not surprising when we recount her post-ESPN amaz-ing life.

> *I was excited to get the job at ESPN. I certainly knew it was an exciting endeavor and I did want to be part of something new. I think I was hired in September 1979. I am pretty sure you were the one who told me to apply.*
>
> *I do know this. I was coming from WFSB-TV in Hartford where I ran studio camera and had had a short stint as on-camera talent for* PM Magazine. *I also was going to be making more money at ESPN than I had at either Channel 3 or CPTV where I had also worked as their still photog-rapher and produced a few of their pledge spots.*
>
> *I believe the salary was $14,000 and at the time, that seemed a lot.*

I think Annette Stovala and I were the first women hired, at least on the production side of things. We met there and became fast friends, if for no other reason than we spent A LOT of time together in that studio.

Both of us recall bringing in sleeping bags to catch a wink under the set between the live studio inserts. Annette became my maid of honor at my wedding to Bob Waller, former voice of the Oakland A's and one of the on-camera sports talent hired that first year.

Bob and I hit it off. He once commented he liked to watch me change lights up in the rafters. Our dates were in the wee hours of the morning at local diners.

ESPN did not treat Bob well. He was under a verbal understanding that he could return to Chicago, where he was living, and work as a field producer. We left for Chicago to follow that plan but it never came to fruition. Bob and I signed on to work at WMAQ-TV in Chicago.

Annette and Mary at a wedding. The bride is in white.
COURTESY MARY WALTON

Although, sadly, our marriage did not last, I am proud to say we worked as a team to produce an award-winning documentary, If Not Today, Then Tomorrow, *on the effects of brain trauma on boxers.*

You had asked Annette what it felt like to work in such a testosterone-filled environment. Both of us do not remember it that way. Our memories are filled with lots of laughter, collegial good times and with the crazy hours things like Thanksgiving in the hallway.

I have a particular crazy memory of shooting with pistols in the middle of the night outside in the fields surrounding ESPN. Don't ask me who brought the firearms. I just remember shooting at cans placed on a fence.

We were all young and simply having too much fun to feel we were in any way competitive with each other. I also remember a certain security guard that was quite fearful of the giant satellite dish outside our facility. He harbored concerns that he could become ill or at the very least alert aliens of our existence.

Mary went on to win an Emmy for *Fastbreak to Glory, the DuSable Panthers*, an original televised play about legendary Jim Brown's coaching of the first all-Black high school team in 1954 to reach the Illinois state championship.

She has gone on to work on advance teams for President Clinton, and other callings that if she was any other personality I'd say were courageous.

But, for Mary, taking 180-degree career turns is perfectly normal. Today she is a licensed marital and family therapist and in a typically Mary Walton way, she is an occasional coxswain or frequent third-seat rower in a quad shell for the Newport Seabase rowing club, traveling the world with shell mates to events like the bucket list Venice Vogalonga rowers competition.

Annette Stavola became an emergency engineering team substitute hours after launch crews realized it might be inhumane to ask their team to keep ESPN on the air, once we started, for nearly round-the-clock telecasts.

She came from Connecticut Public Television and became a *SportsCenter* stabilizer and ended up running camera with Mary, and enjoyed revisiting hijinks and talent workarounds this way:

Let me preface this with memories have dimmed over time but some are vivid, and while specifics may have fallen into dim categories, anecdotes, people, and vibe remain strong.

A Connecticut native, I had never been to Bristol until the day ESPN went on the air and I was called in by a Connecticut Public Television work friend to relieve them from their master control duties. They had been on the air for hours and there wasn't anyone there to relieve them.

I knew they had changed jobs and went with this new sports cable company which was paying a lot more than our current salary. I said sure I would be right over, what better way to get a foot in the door. I had no idea what was in store at ESPN from that day forward nor did most of the staff working there.

I believe even management did not know the magnitude of 24 hours a day, seven days a week on air would have on all of us, as well as our viewers. It was and remains the quintessential "startup."

Arriving in Bristol, without GPS, my directions were:

"Just look for the big satellite dish you can't miss it. The mobile unit is behind the construction, in the back dirt lot, to the left of the porta-potties."

I walked into the unit . . . said my hellos to my friend and sat down to master control. It was one unit, two tiers, and was introduced around.

Scotty Connal and Chet Simmons were standing in the control room where they would drift in and out over the duration of the time we spent in the mobile unit. This was a very hands-on approach.

There were no run sheets. I asked when we would go to breaks and studio.

"When the tape runs out. . . . or we run out of programming."

It was then that it hit home I was a far cry from Sesame Street.

I got my foot in the door and was hired shortly thereafter as a tech/cameraperson.

They doubled my salary from public television. I was two years out of college and this was a big deal. Granted sports was not my forte, but I had gotten thorough training at CPTV in all aspects of TV. It was an extension of my education and it was new and everyone was young and it was anything goes to make this work.

We made it up as we went along. Win. Win. Win.

The people made working there an adventure, we didn't realize how groundbreaking it was. We just had to find a way to man a 24-hour network and keep it going.

I had no part in finding the programming, sales, or monies to pay us all. I just did the day to day of light, cameras, switching, audio, basically helping us stay on the air without too many glitches.

There were so many young people there, we kept each other going. Life-long friendships were formed in the wee hours between SportsCenters.

We all worked for the greater good, there wasn't room or time for anything else.

The mobile truck which was ESPN master control while the rest of the studio was being built was the heart of the network until the switcher died and we had to get the new control room up and running during a segment of tape. We never got a full fax check on it until it went to use.

Thank God the technical staff, who built ESPN studios and facilities from the ground up, were the best. The control room worked, and we were out of the truck.

Once I became a cameraperson my cohort was another woman, Mary Walton. I'm sure we had a third camera but it may have been a locked-down shot as I don't remember anyone else. There weren't enough bodies.

We ran those nightly SportsCenter *cameras. I worked 90 days straight once we went 24/7. After the 2:30 a.m.* SportsCenter *we would meet in the parking lot for refreshments provided by either Chuckles Pagano or Boomer Chris Berman or Fred Muzzy our infamous and class cut-up early-days directors.*

Instead of heading home Mary and I would get a few hours of shut-eye under the SportsCenter *set. We had brought sleeping bags.*

Many mornings Jim Rosenberg or some other thoughtful suit would bring in coffee and donuts for our wakeup call, then onto the next day's SportsCenter.

Luckily by that time we had ridded the studio of the skunk that had made anchors' eyes water during a show even though the actual skunk had been ushered out. Often flies would distract talent during the broadcast.

Fortunately there weren't teleprompters so the talent only had to ad lib until the fly was out of our viewfinders. We couldn't keep up with the swatting, so we hung flypaper.

Some days we had a stage manager, some days Mary and I would fill in the slot behind the camera. On one of those days Lee Leonard and Bob Waller were deep in discussion on the set. We gave them a countdown to air: "One minute." "Thirty seconds!" Yelling louder "three, two, one!"

Otherworldly Fred Muzzy and Annette Stavola

Bob was reclining with his feet on the desk, Lee with loosened tie looked at us and asked "are we on the air?"

We nodded YES vigorously.

Bob laughed, "Is this a joke?"

This time we shook our heads NO!

Unperturbed, it seemed and laughing while they were at it, Lee straightened his tie, Bob sat up straight and said, "Oh, we are on the air . . . welcome to SportsCenter.*"*

We worked during that first Thanksgiving and decided to have Thanksgiving dinner in the hallway. Someone brought a turkey and others filled in the blanks. Thankfully we had a meal. This became one of ESPN's traditions. We were a family.

ESPN was desperate for programming and filler material. You could never plan how long a live sports telecast might last, so we had different length fillers for everything.

If you had an idea, you could grab a camera setup and off you would go to shoot and edit it. Mary and I did just that for the Harvard-Yale game. One of the problems for ESPN in the early days was press credentials. No one knew who or what we were. Since we weren't getting any credentials we decided to just shoot the tailgating and that became our filler.

We didn't have too much fun taping it, did we?

I wish I had the raw footage but the highly edited version aired, a lot!

It has been often asked of me, How was is it working in a male-dominated sports network back then? I never thought of it that way.

I never felt they thought of me as a female television technician. They needed people who would commit to a crazy new enterprise who were willing to do what it took to keep us on the air.

There were a handful of other women in other departments, some with better jobs, more experience, older, but we were friendly. We banded together male and female because we were in the trenches together and that makes some strange partnerships.

If we were breaking those glass ceilings in the early days, we were unaware. Maybe that's what brought us all together. Maybe that's what made us a family.

Annette Stavola became Annette Stavola Leisure, marrying now former ESPN vice president of international programming, Tim Leisure.

Annette continues to provide her talents at high-end events, at this writing offering a world of sports television experience at Wimbledon.

There's a third woman who like Mary and Annette helped hold *SportsCenter* together with duct tape, cardboard, and maybe a bobby pin, but she'd have had to borrow the pin from someone else I expect.

She is **Jan Hayes,** and Jan is one fine friend, if your fettle is fine.

Our time harkens to that Hot L Baltimore amateur production that Mary produced and starred in and I slept through as a lobby prop.

Jan Hayes
COURTESY MARY WALTON

Jan built the set for that production, and her adept brandishing of a skill saw and vision to hear out the producer's set design whim, and then go about making it better her way, was a blast to watch.

I was immediately drawn to Jan's ingenuity and called on it in a freelance job that was to celebrate the 25th anniversary of Connecticut School of Broadcasting, a client.

Making a big show of the school's founder Dick Robinson's radio pedigree, we decided to leverage his Farmington mansion's recording studio during World Series weekend.

We put former New York baseball Giants broadcasting teammates Marty Glickman and Johnny Most in the studio with a monitor, to re-create the sound effects and the way announcers who could not travel with their home team would call the game by reading game notes fed back to them by tickertape.

Jan and her significant other Walter built individual and operating crystal radio sets for this extravaganza celebrating radio history, and they were mailed as invites to media.

I didn't have to explain or ask, just showed Jan a picture and her questions aptly were:

How many? How soon? How much is your budget?

She put the same smart, Irish, frill-free ethic to work in the upstairs version of *SportsCenter*, where in the mayhem of putting together multiple shows a night she kept the frenzy under a semblance of control.

With an innate eye that seemed to anticipate a need, Jan Hayes appeared clairvoyant at times, and in the earliest of *SportsCenter*s was a not-so-quiet glue.

Jan went on to stage a marquee full of famous productions as back-of-the-house director of the Bushnell Performing Arts Center, while surely maintaining her sweet sting of confidence.

CHAPTER 8

Mad Men and Porn

WHEN BILL RASMUSSEN HIRED BOB CHAMBERLAIN AND ME, A PAIR OF ad men from opposite sides of the Connecticut version of Madison Avenue, sparks ensued, lighting absurd and historic advertising and programming fires.

Bob had just spent 24 cushy years with insurance giant Connecticut General, ultimately enjoying the client side perks of a multimillion-dollar budget to spread around.

I'd relieved myself of the stressors of building a from-scratch street-smart ad agency which went on to become one of the market's creative leaders, at a personal expense I tried to soothe by dousing with Scottish imports.

Bob joined not many days after Lou Palmer and I crossed the Plainville ESPN threshold.

One of cable television's historic advertising stories, replete with not-so-funny chapters, is the epic Anheuser-Busch exclusive beer commercial agreement that began as a brainstorm between us in the United Cable building attic.

Who's the bigger advertiser, Schlitz or Budweiser?

Might have been a dead heat then, Schlitz supporting its Leo Burnett–created "Go for the Gusto" campaign and Budweiser telling fans "This Bud's for You."

The long-admired Leo Burnett advertising agency was where a former colleague of mine worked, so I volunteered to begin mining that prospect. I said *colleague,* not *friend,* and barely could get a message returned, not to mention a door opened.

On the other hand Bob leveraged his Darcy McManus influence, and sure enough Gene Petrillo, the agency's Budweiser brand manager, was on the phone to us. Gene Petrillo quarterbacked the signing of a multimillion-dollar exclusive beer category contract that Anheuser-Busch dominated ESPN programming with for five years.

This chapter, however, goes on to celebrate Gene Petrillo's vision that began months before ESPN ever launched. Elsewhere I blogged that Gene should posthumously be given a Guts in Advertising Award.

Here it is:

Guts in Advertising Award
By Peter Fox

Eugene A. Petrillo is hereby nominated by me for a posthumous Guts-In-Advertising trophy.

The story in a moment, but first:

Since SportsEdTV recruited me to pitch in with their effort to become the ESPN of sports education, I've been reliving moments of the birthing of that sports behemoth where I had a birds eye view as its founding executive producer.

Regaled in many media are the swashbuckling pioneers who bled sports to get ESPN started, but some of the silent suits in that story have never received the kudos they should.

That's what got me thinking about Gene Petrillo, Executive Vice President Advertising of Darcy, McManus, Masius the powerful agency which served beer giant Anheuser-Busch.

It was Gene whose guts and vision earned his client exclusive-in-beer-category ads for a year and which also bought an avalanche of commercial spots and billboards daily.

So, fast-forward and here we are: Digits. Streaming. Cell phones and towers. GPS. SEO AI. Et al.

Still, it's a battle for eyes and attitudes for marketers. A good dose of Gene Petrillo vision and intuition will serve you well if you're hoping to sniff out an early stage company to ride to mutual successes.

Let's fold some data around what the good deal looked like:

- *Anheuser-Busch pays ESPN $1,380,000 or in today's money $5,423,400 using a 3.93 factor.*

- *ESPN broadcasts three 30 second commercials an hour, 24 hours a day, 365 days and adds merchandising billboards or 29,280+ exclusive beer messages to ESPN's audience.*

- *1979 ESPN reaches just under 6 million homes; 2020 it is plus 90 million.*

So to get a handle on worth consider:

- *A 1978 Superbowl commercial with 7,894,000 viewers cost $162,300*

- *A 2020 Superbowl commercial with 90,000,000 viewers cost $5.600,000*

Beyond any arithmetic contortions there's always a narrative and that's what I witnessed.

ESPN's Bob Chamberlain was a former client of Gene Petrillo and got the conversation going that led to the big Budweiser deal and this nomination.

Before the Budweiser deal jelled, we sought to get a guerilla style backup conversation going with Schlitz Beer's ad folks at Leo Burnett. We pretty much got stonewalled there, as they focused on prepping their Go for the Gusto *Olympics sponsorship.*

Well, when I tell this story it usually ends up with a sass that asks:

When's the last time you had a Schlitz?

Are there any Gene Petrillos lurking in the world of sports marketing?

Bob Chamberlain gets bragging rights on that one.

The day he came bursting into our production area exclaiming "I just got darts" is one of my favorite funny Chamberlain memories.

But the one I remember most was the Easter 1979 weekend when he harebrained a way for us to televise the tennis finals of the Grand Prix World Cup Tennis Tournament in Monaco as a demonstration of our international clout to the cable industry.

Ha! We couldn't get time on the international television satellite. It seems they didn't recognize who or what we were and by the time we got that issue solved it was too late.

So, Bob and Scott Rasmussen went to Monaco and each of the weekend days when the competition was over, took raw international footage with wild sound and no French announcers in large two-inch videotape canisters and raced to the Paris airport and put it on the Concorde, bound for JFK Airport in New York.

After hiring a customs broker, a position I think should have a different name, the delivery of the Saturday tapes from the Concorde to customs, then the broker to me, was velvet smooth.

I rented New York's WPIX production facilities with the help of HBO's sports director Marty Glickman, who'd become a silent mentor in some ways. Lou Palmer met me there, and in a magic couple of hours ESPN broadcast flawless same-day television of the Monaco Grand Prix, with Lou Palmer's genius making it sound like we were there.

From WPIX we sent a signal to RCA's Vernon Valley uplink to ESPN's transponder 7 and *voilà*, we were international broadcasters . . . sort of.

Though Saturday was velvet, Sunday's finals between Vitas Gerulaitis and Bjorn Borg went too long for comfort and Scott had to race to the Concorde. He made it, but on my end it got just as nerve wracking.

It seems the nice-guy customs agent of Saturday was replaced by his opposite on Sunday and "it seemed" there was a problem with the videotape canisters. I was told the customs official who'd inspected them thought they were pornography!

A hundred-dollar bill fell out of my pocket as I headed to the bathroom. Somehow the customs agent had convinced the inspector to trust the freckle-faced rookie who didn't know about clearing videotapes, and my booty was retrieved, and my other booty was unslung.

WPIX and Lou did their repeat and I shook my fist at Bob Chamberlain.

Bob left ESPN in the Evey evicts. He joined our mutual friend Eric Hansen in a timely and shrewd idea to market the twice-an-hour local cable system breaks we and other networks offered.

And then Bob's big-for-his-britches spending bankrupted their partnership, and I've never forgave him for doing that to Eric, resilient as he is.

THE IMMORTAL RICK WEITERMAN

A straight version of the Rick Weiterman story would say that he was the first athlete ever to be shown competing live on ESPN.

That would exclude UConn's senior center Jeff Carr, who jumped center on the network's November 17, 1978, first demonstration telecast, prior to the network signing on full-time with Rick Weiterman tossing the first pitch in the Slow Pitch World Series on September 7, 1979, 295 days after Jeff tipped to budding UConn superstar Corny Thompson.

Schlitz softball pitcher Rick Weiterman
COURTESY SLOW PITCH SOFTBALL

Jeff Carr's tip is confined to a historic solitary, but Rick Weiterman's isn't for all the wrong reasons.

In the crowded launch control room that first ESPN evening stood a Budweiser pride led by Darcy McManus Budweiser visionaries Gene Petrillo and Dick Simon, all flushed with anticipation like the rest of us. Gene's steering of the exclusive $1.3 million Anheuser-Busch dollars to us earned his team's invite to the delivery room at ESPN's birth.

As our first live sports event swung into motion, the Slow Pitch World Series, an amazing pall swept over the room as our camera zoomed onto a close shot of Weiterman, sporting the loud logo of SCHLITZ across his chest!

ESPN's inaugural telecast would become the Kentucky Bourbons versus the Milwaukee Schlitz, brought to you by Budweiser!

Damn!

What sort of advertising demon had pitched an underhanded curse to our euphoria?

After blanching nervously, Chet Simmons, Bill, and Scott were let off the hook by a gracious Gene Petrillo, who smiled away the mischievous destiny of sports, another reason why I remember his class act.

CHAPTER 9

Naughty

SPORTS GAMBLING FOR ME HAS ALWAYS BEEN A DISTASTEFUL SUBJECT. It's an argument I always lose, but I know I'm right. It spoils and corrupts.

Please don't look for my Roman collar. It ain't there. I don't believe relying on your own skills in sports is gambling. It is betting on something I control, my play. I have golfed and won thousands of dollars. And still get off on kicking your ass for five bucks.

Gambling at ESPN, especially in the beginning was water-cooler banter. Note, the water cooler didn't exist during the earliest days.

Before I climb the last couple of steps to my anti-gambling pulpit, I have to confirm the story of Bob Pronovost's money-where-his-mouth-is skill bet. Bob told me it came out of the formulaic boredom of producing and directing *SportsCenter* highlights programs late into the evening, which were mostly score reading.

It seems, Bob, no stranger to a little swagger, mused that he could direct the show, calling screens, cameras, and video, upside down and backward off the reflection of content screens on the inverted glass of the control room's back glass wall.

Taunting calls to Bob's braggadocio resulted in a good wager, and that evening he delivered and won! I love athletes like Bob, Namath, MJ, Ali, and Teddy Ballgame.

Back in my pulpit, I suppose my disdain comes from witnessing point shaving in my Jimmy Olsen sportswriting time with the *Norwich Bulletin*, covering UConn's Hugh Greer –coached 1960–1961 basketball team that was implicated in a widespread syndicate of organized cheating.

Greer was heartbroken as players of his were implicated. I lost my crew-cut high-burns virginity. Today, with the proliferation of sports books and online betting, I've lost, but go down tattling.

SportsCenter as I experienced it in the early days was a haven. Bob, and his other sidekick, Steve Bogart, of Humphrey and Lauren direct lineage, worked with us at WFSB and were high profile about their betting. Bogart has gone Howard Hughes for this recounting, though I can find no reports of obsessive hand washing.

Before the internet, *SportsCenter* enjoyed unique access into professional sports locker rooms. Do you suppose injury information, or maybe a pitching change, not elsewhere known might provide gamblers' heavenly manna: an edge?

Perhaps distracted by Dewar's, I missed most of the other ESPN gambling chatter, but Michael Freeman didn't when he wrote about ESPN, saying "Gambling permeated the network to such a degree that ESPN attracted the attention of the Connecticut State Police."

"After a series of raids across Connecticut in the early 1980s investigators with the organized crime unit noticed a high number of calls from ESPN's offices to bookmakers around the state. Antigambling unit officials contacted ESPN management warning them to control their employees or there would be arrests, according to ESPN officials," Freeman added.

Current irony abounds as ESPN's online gambling advertising seem to be as important to them today as beer was then. Moreover, as I write this, ESPN is announcing a 10-year deal with a casino company to create an online sports betting brand called ESPN Bet.

Well, so much for that personal disdain for online sports betting. With the overwhelming online promotion of media betting, how long will it be until you can get a local app that posts a line on your daughter's high school soccer game?

And how much will you bet? And how much might she make to slough off on a couple of scoring opportunities?

SEX

Sex, now that's a different story.

The hookup culture that COVID-19 put a damper on was in full flower in ESPN's infancy. Think about it, a crew of young people recruited for their talent and affordability tossed together in a new town, working overtime into the black of the night, mostly unsupervised by upper management.

Sexy stories abound, most of which remain vague through me too eyes, though the white knight chivalrous action that put a stop to a knucklehead's not-so-consensual grab-ass of a lady 'SPNaut is noted, given the you-know-who-you-are jerk ought to be locker slammed and was.

Another I wouldn't tell unless he was in repose, but one big-time executive's desk was definitely besmirched with buttock prints of a traditionally engaged pair.

Romance, of the not naughty kind, is celebrated in its own space here, as it did have a fluency of its own. When I think of the late-night *SportsCenter* ESPN crew signing off for the day an hour or so after the West Coast games, and the void in the middle of the East Coast night, it makes sense that romance and mischief would follow.

Mischief manifested in parking lot beer binges and even target shooting that surprisingly didn't attract visits from Officer Friendly et al. Mary Walton distinctly remembers shooting pistols at cans in the back of the studio after sign-off, though she can't implicate the gunrunner.

There was party time, whatever the excuse. In fact some of the crew, working the excruciating hours, figured out how to cut down on commuting time and increase party time by renting apartments in what is sort of fondly remembered as Edit 4—Edit 3 being Hamps bar and den of iniquity.

Edit 4, as we called the barracks-like compound directly across the street from our original studio, also offered more than hotbedding by early and late shifts, and allowed for downtime strolls across the street for tokes and libation. As for off hours, Edit 4 rocked, often to the discomfort of neighbors, so often we just invited them. Some enjoyed.

What doesn't seem to fit elsewhere is a Glenn Close in *Fatal Attraction*–like over-the-top attachment that was emotionally difficult for me via my connection with the attachee.

"ESPN Edit Suite #4" 916–924 Middle Street, Bristol, Connecticut

I'm not privy to the origins, but one woman who came to us in the tsunami of NBC and New York television folks got so emotionally entwined with one of the several early recruits that I had developed that it turned out to be pretty wobbly for her and especially me one night.

To say she became distraught when rebuffed would be an understatement. When she called me to her home, in a calming effort I visited, knowing we'd share the fifth of Cutty Sark I had already nipped. She was an otherwise talented and interesting person.

Arriving at her complex, I tripped over a wheel stop, rolling like the athlete I am, to protect the Cutty Sark, tucking it under my arm like Jim Brown and taking the macadam's blow with my shoulder and face.

It changed the subject, nursing my bloody face. We never spoke of her not-so-magnificent obsession. Instead, it became the trigger to my ESPN exit and first of two rehab stints.

I was not the only one with a substance abuse problem in those early days. Bolivian marching powder residue was sometimes found on flat surfaces in makeup areas and restrooms, and sniffles falsely attributed to the change in the seasons were not uncommon.

CHAPTER 10

Afterglow

ON OCTOBER 15, 1979, WHEN BILL RASMUSSEN—THE JOHN GLENN OF ESPN—celebrated his 47th birthday, the earliest 'SPNaut team got together to mark the day.

It was sweet with a taste of bitter.

The afterglow of launch and the importance of ESPN's birthing that we had nursed through pre- and now postnatal days continued to wash over us, but impending Evey and Simmons clouds flew in front of our sun intermittently.

All that said, it was a Bill Rasmussen moment, and our believers had a lot to say:

Guy Wilson said "experiencing this experience with you has been an experience!"

Gordie and Colleen Howe wrote "Happy Birthday to a Superstar" on the giant card where we all left wishes. UConn's John Toner wrote, "It's a short time—but a long way—from umpire to running back, Mr. Chairman."

George Conner said, "Bill Rasmussen . . . the man with an idea . . . a dream . . . who never doubted it would be done. A personal pleasure to know him."

But, extant of another Guy Wilson anecdote that flushed every cheek in the room, Mike Caruso's gifted and spot-on sketch of the birthday boy was accompanied by a written tribute we'd all hear.

It's below, only to be upstaged by another to follow:

WHAT'S A BILL RASMUSSEN?
By Mike Caruso

With all the aplomb and derring-do of an adventurous base-runner who seeks to win a ball game with a dash of courage, Bill Rasmussen has stolen home plate again.

The Ty Cobb of the television industry is performing with the same determined, dexterous manner he effected on Midwestern diamonds nearly three decades ago as a semiprofessional baseball player.

A concept born of a traffic delay during a drive to his daughter's 16th birthday party turned into a wild and crazy expedition into the world of video that has made unbelievable, rapid strides toward fruition.

Rasmussen's idea wasn't geared for a short run. It survived because of innovation, a bit of tradition and no tricks. It was a process of things falling into place at the right time.

The result? A satellite sports service with the ultimate promise of around-the-clock athletes in action for the sports buff. And there is plenty of that variety longing for the 24-hour beam that's tailored to their preference.

William F. Rasmussen's history began 46 years ago on the South Side of Chicago. While playing third base between high school studies, his hot corner act caught the fancy of a Detroit Tigers scout but big league beckoning never materialized. Instead, he chose little DePauw University in Greencastle, Indiana, to pursue academics.

A hitch with the U.S. Air Force followed DePauw. During his service stint, Bill's wife, Lois, introduced Scott, the first of their three children, to life. Second son Glenn and daughter Lynn made later arrivals.

Bill got a taste of marketing for Westinghouse in New Jersey after leaving the Air Force and his experience in that field led to his cofounding of Ad-Aid, a mail order clearinghouse that serviced Westinghouse deliveries for the most part.

In the interim, he was awarded a master's degree in business administration from Rutgers University.

He began warming up to his niche when he took a job as sports director at radio station WTTT in the Massachusetts college town of Amherst.

Bill Rasmussen Sketch by Mike Caruso

Rasmussen created a New England sports radio network, a parcel of University of Massachusetts athletic events, and toiled in turn for channels 22 and 40 in nearby Springfield as a meteorologist, sportscaster and news director.

In 1974, he moved to the New England Whalers hockey team as communications director and play by-play announcer for broadcasts and telecasts.

Meanwhile, Scott, who did a commercial when he was eight for a minor league baseball club and at 14 teamed with his father in presenting a schoolboy hockey tournament, freelanced for the Whalers in various capacities.

The Rasmussens initially considered cable sports programming during their participation in the promotion and production of hockey immortal Gordie Howe's 50th birthday gala in March 1978.

Three months later, they hosted their first media conference at the offices of what was to be their first affiliate, United Cable of Plainville, Connecticut. And they named their creation the Entertainment and Sports Programming Network:

Discussions, conferences and negotiations of all sorts ensued.

Thirteen months ago, the Rasmussens were held up in a traffic jam on their way to a family birthday party in Ocean Grove, New Jersey.

Somehow, all the preliminary planning—site, construction, mobile units, continuous and total sports network—evolved from a conversation in a car during a traffic stall on a hot August day.

Setting up temporary headquarters in United Cable's Plainville offices, beating a time expiration for the Transponder no. 7 berth aboard the RCA Satcom I satellite, financial considerations, a University of Connecticut sports package, inaugural presentation and acquiring personnel became milestones.

Perhaps the most vital coup was an agreement with the National Collegiate Athletic Association to telecast its championship season, an assortment of regular season, conference and championship events in 18 different sports of the three NCAA divisions. It meant making more than 700 events available for Gus Q. Fan's viewing via ESPN's cable affiliates.

Multiple system operators began signing on and United Cable, appropriately, headed the list.

Last November, the University of Connecticut Athletes in Action basketball game at Storrs, CT, was ESPN's baptismal screening effort.

Happenings were fast and frequent.

Ground was broken to start construction at ESPN's permanent site at Bristol, CT, in March, Anheuser-Busch made the largest single cable advertising purchase ever (ESPN's first) in May, and four and a half months ago Getty Oil Company exercised an option to buy 85 percent of ESPN.

The Getty-backed ESPN express put a top-flight engineer at the throttle in late July when it named Chester R. (Chet) Simmons, former president of NBC Sports, the head of operations. Bill Rasmussen took on the newly-created role of chairman of the board.

About the time the 10 meter transmitter and receiver "soup bowls" were installed at the Bristol site, Allan B. (Scotty) Connal, a 32-year NBC veteran and former vice-president of sports operations for that network, joined Simmons at ESPN as senior vice-president-operations/productions.

September 7 was ESPN's D-Day. The brash newcomer on the video block blossomed out with an engaging array of athletes and athletics to more than four million homes through 600+ systems.

The opening month featured the American Professional Slo-Pitch League softball World Series, the Federation Internationale de Lutte Amateur (FILA wrestling championships) from San Diego, U.S. Invitational Volleyball (men's and women's finals) from Colorado Springs, and the Davis Cup American Zone tennis finals between Argentina and the U.S. at Memphis. Hurling from Ireland, IKF Kart Racing and amateur tournaments of American Legion Baseball and the National Baseball Congress also highlighted September scheduling.

Of course, NCAA football and soccer games played a big part.

Gridiron offerings listed the Grambling-Morgan State clash at Yankee Stadium, Southern Cal at LSU, Arizona State at Florida State and Notre Dame at Purdue.

Soccer enthusiasts readily recognized UCLA at St. Louis, SIU (Edwardsville) at San Francisco and Duke at Clemson as classic match-ups.

Developing a growing level of advertising revenue by offering continuous quality sports programming, reaching audiences in affluent, better-educated "achiever" households through television without the waste of broadcast networks, an advertising buy at low dollar cost, and a franchise with future growth in value have been established as ESPN's marketing strategy.

Cable is a youngster that knows no bounds. And ESPN has added to the phenomenon. That's why Bill Rasmussen is confident that when the reviews from the recliners are in, ESPN will spell success.

When Rasmussen played in a semipro baseball circuit he stole home not once but four times in a single season.

The success of a daring, a venture earned, a venture gained!

Mike Caruso, a Buffalo Bills PR veteran, central casting newspaper curmudgeon, and dad to eleven Carusos of varying sizes and ages, hid a lot of things beneath a stocky presence, his artistic touch, and his word-smithing, including his way with people.

Mike's telling of Bill Rasmussen's fancy flight could only have been upstaged in that melancholy moment while unspoken trepidation filled

Lois Rasmussen's birthday love letter to Bill
COURTESY GEOFFREY BRAY

the hearts of celebrating 'SPNauts by Bill's wife Lois, her quiet yet stoic love expressed ever so sweetly in a birthday card to Bill.

In the weeks and months that followed, afterglow faded and startup hangover began to permeate the upper levels of the '78 'SPNauts. Bill resigned, and in his words, described our situation as especially difficult.

In *Sports Junkies Rejoice,* Bill wrote:

The days immediately following launch were especially difficult for the original employees, including myself. On the Sunday following the launch, Simmons, Evey and I had breakfast. During that brief meeting, Evey in no uncertain terms told me "Chet's in charge. Stay out of the way."

A week later Simmons informed Scott that Evey wanted to talk to him. Scott called Getty's headquarters and was invited to come to Los Angeles to "discuss his future with ESPN."

Some future! Some offer! Evey's offer to Scott was a 75 percent cut in pay to stay with the company and learn the business from the bottom up. Scott was gone by October 1.

The same pattern applied to other "originals." Bob Bray was offered a new post at 50% of his former salary. John Foley was terminated in November by "mutual agreement." Bob Chamberlain was not even given the courtesy of an offer. He was just terminated.

Peter Fox and I lasted about a year. The standard offer didn't work very well with us, but eventually we succumbed and resigned. The same is true of Bob Ronstrom. My brother Don stayed on through January 1980 before he submitted his resignation.

Lou Palmer was the only survivor and at this writing is still doing a strong professional job for the network.

Bill's words spoke to the handful of '78 'SPNauts who tripped over each other in the founding downstairs rented offices of Plainville's United Cable building.

When the rocket lifted off with Getty fuel, '78 and some '79 'SPNaut crew populated the rented attic of the same building, and many became strong and long-term stalwarts of the network, without whom the impossible would not have become a transformative television icon.

Those of us with higher profiles couldn't duck the swing of new corporate scythes.

CHAPTER 11

Homegrown and Other Presidents

UNABLE TO SPORT THE EUPHEMISTIC AND ARBITRARILY ASSIGNED 'SPNaut brand which '78 & '79ers earned, George Bodenheimer is a mirror of the ESPN phenomena, and is thus entitled to the honorary designation of 'SPNaut should he choose.

As the 150th employee of ESPN, the economics-degreed Bodenheimer took an $8,000-a-year job that would equate to $4 an hour if he ever worked 40 weekly hours. Ha!

George jumped at the offer because he had a sports dream and was ignored by big leagues and big venues where he applied.

Into the mailroom he went and back and forth to New York and Connecticut airports ferrying famous and infamous headed to Bristol, nowhere Connecticut. Though a marketing DNA was inherent, George's trip through the earliest of ESPN days included stints in the library, the studio as cameraman and floor manager, but most delightfully as driver to iconic Dick Vitale.

The Scotty Connal/Greenwich axis continued with George's hiring. In junior high school Scotty had been George's hockey coach.

Marketing embers got George out of the production side and into spreading the gospel of ESPN when he read of a Dallas job opening to add cable systems. Off he went to the South where George Bodenheimer found ESPN's secret sauce talking to mom-and-pop cable operators in small towns.

In his book *Every Town Is a Sports Town*, George paraphrases conversations he'd hear over and over that set the premise for his continued rise to ESPN's presidency.

"Gee, the idea of a twenty-four-hour sports channel is kind of nutty," they'd say. "But, we'll carry it, because, you know, George, this is a sports town."

So, ascending through the creative culture that is ESPN, George took to heart what he learned in the 'burbs, backlots, and sandlots, that sports is a culture, a language and a passion that had no color, religion, or politics then.

Today? Not so much.

Another homegrown ESPN president preceded George; Steve Bornstein began in January of 1980, and was interviewed in December of '79 so another arbitrary anointment as an 'SPNaut is given.

Steve joined as a program coordinator, sort of like the final job assigned to me before the tedious work began triggering extended lunches at Ray Smith's garden of gin and grins.

The Bornstein buildup was a full-fledged reflection of the 'SPNaut pedigree he earned the hard way. On Steve's watch he steered the ESPN rocket through radio, magazine, and internet spaces.

Beyond the Rasmussen and Simmons presidencies, at first an unsteady Stu Evey played the big business card and went to CBS to haul in Bill Grimes.

Grimes turned ESPN profitable, by performing a ballsy marketing coup when he stopped offering ESPN as a freebie to the cable industry and began charging them for carriage.

By then, tractor pulls, arm wrestling, and caber tossing had morphed into whip-around-coverage of NCAA basketball, Sunday Night NFL Football, MLB games, and NHL games, and subscribers would have raised all sorts of hell if cable operators cut the ESPN sports umbilical.

Grimes hired a McKinsey consultant, Roger Werner, to become chief operating officer, and later Roger ascended when Grimes vacated.

Though Roger Werner's role as president seemed without major innovation, he stabilized the rocket and minted money to the tune of a reported $600 million in sales and $150 million in profits.

Some kind of gusher, eh, Stu?

By then, Getty had sold to Texaco and Texaco had bailed to ABC.

Other honorary 'SPNaut markings should be accorded to presidential nurturers John Skipper and Jimmy Pitaro.

I have never met former ESPN president John Skipper, though I share a recovery kinship with a man who quietly fought addiction and knew enough to do something about it, resigning in a graceful way to attend to his personal need.

On John's watch sports television rights ballooned. He closed a nine-year, $12 billion NBA deal and a $7.3 billion deal for the college football playoffs.

Those numbers make me think of that measly $1.3 million, one-year exclusive beer advertising contract that Schlitz didn't take. When's the last time you had one?

Jimmy Pitaro is now at the top of the chain of the Disney-owned ESPN. He's overseeing the swinging of a big corporate scythe, as a reported 15 percent will be cut.

An effort to interview Jimmy Pitaro evoked this response from the gatekeepers:

"Unfortunately, Jimmy does very few interviews and even less book interviews. Since he is so far removed from 1979, I doubt he would do this."

Not the same gatekeepers that kept ESPN architect Geoff Bray and I from visiting the building he built and I helped design, but of the same ilk.

CHAPTER 12

Ground Control

THOSE OF US SPORTING 'SPNAUT WINGS COULD HARDLY HAVE DONE SO without equally important, hard-charging members of the ground control crews that rocketed ESPN programming into geosynchronous orbit on RCA's Satcom I satellite, revolutionizing sports television forever.

The 'SPNaut Ground Control Team is a concoction of the author. Its membership is comprised of support personnel entitled to wear the coveted Orange Oval.

As this work took form, it became painfully apparent that many worthy stories would go untold, especially those of passionate folks who quietly supported headliners of the epic ESPN birth.

'SPNaut Ground Control

Many have been previously mentioned and justifiably ought to have an orange oval ceded to their story. Some provided ground control support as employees, others as vendors. And still more as freelancers.

Best efforts have been made to embrace those who had touched in some way the pre- and postnatal periods of ESPN's birth, from its 1978 beginnings to the 1980 toddler time.

For the purpose of presenting Orange Ovals, the names that are assembled here come from an array of sources.

From 1978 demo events, I remember Garrett Schenck, Arnold Dean, Paul Pac, Lynn Bermingham, Allen Allshouse, Randy Scalise, Scott Gray, Arnold Dean, and Dee Rowe.

And from the bizarre days putting a network on the air from trailers parked in a muddy construction site, and a half-built broadcast building, come the all-knowing, all-smiling front desk and switchboard greetings of Carol Pelletier.

As top-line consultants, Clay Ackerson and Til Ferdenzi are highlighted in the very first edition of *ESPN Uplink*, February 1, 1980, as are several ground controllers newly added to the crew:

Among those ground controllers were Annette Leiderman, Patti Nolan, Mark Schumacher Sr., Rod Lane, Rhonda Lane, Paul DiPietro, John Cistulli, Peter Sumpf, John Kaszycki, Joann Crowthers, Victoria Haggerty, Mark Anderson, Richard Pizzoni, Jane Himmelstein, Kyra Skrkypek, John Baron, Al Maiorano, Michael Hull, Gabriel Osho, Lee Franco, Kathy Cowan, Don Levy, Richard McDowell, Marth Ehrlich, Ann-Marie Gray, Dale Reynolds, Joan Izzi, Leslie Howlett, Roger Williams, Laurene Doucette, Mary Imperator, Vin Crowder, Russ Brown, Joe Valerio, and Bob Greenway.

Vol. I No. I
February 1980

The Monthly Newsletter of the Total Sports Cable Network

ESPN Uplink newsletter banner, Volume 1
COURTESY PHIL KULAS

Superstar ESPN historian Phil Kulas

Phil Kulas provided the names of more 'SPNaut ground controllers: Mary Angst, Anne Baily, Jackie Bracco, Dom Camisa, Frank Casarella, Mark Ceglarski, John Cistulli, Al DiPrato, Joe Franco, Deb George, Dave Gleason, Richard Sweet, Dian Sbordone, Julie Paradis, Andre Allen, Steve Anderson, Mark Augustine, Fran Panzo, Bob Paolitto, Jody Patrovsky, Rich Pizoni, Barry Rahmy, Fred Rosenberg, Keith Sandler, Ken Schneider, Don Skinner, Joanne Smith, Judy Smith, Sharon Smith, Ed Sopelak, Bernard Stewart, Holly St. Lifer, Reggie Thomas, Ray Tipton, Mike Boissoneault, Greg Borbas, Rich Capolla, Donna Cullen, Rich Deutsch, Mary Driscoll, Ales Fraser, Dave Grossman, Bull Gutman, Tom Hagel, Vicky Haggerty, Peter Ilowitz, John Kaszychi, Rich Keegan, Libby Ladd, Rose Lorenti, Jeff Winn, Kate Youngdahl, Wimpy Hutchinson, George Gallup.

CHAPTER 13

Family Affair

To SAY EARLY ESPN WAS A FAMILY AFFAIR ISN'T FAIR TO AFFAIRS.

Bill and Scott Rasmussen were founders, and other key leaders and their progeny were key to the disruption of sports television, but that doesn't tell the true story of how tightly knit the earliest 'SPNauts were.

In fact, some children of key ESPN players preceded their parents' involvement. Sherry Simpson, for example, was hired as a production assistant by Jerry Moring for the *SportsCenter* team, a period much before her renowned dad, NBC's Jim Simpson, chose to turn his back on a stellar career there and join ESPN. She remembered it this way:

My father wasn't there when I got hired. He got hired several months later. And I remember at the time there was an article when they did hire him away from NBC, they were saying, Jim Simpson leaves NBC for ESPN, gets a great deal and he even gets his daughter a cushy job at the network as well. And I remember it was like, what the hell?

It gets better:

As Sherry remembers again, the day she got hired she and another interviewee, Chris Petersen, were hired in the Plainville office and Chris offered to drive Sherry to Bristol to see ESPN's studio under construction.

Chris is the son of Getty Oil's president Sid Petersen, who was adamant that he wanted Chris to finish college and *not* take the job at ESPN. Chris had been connected with Compact Video of Los Angeles, the firm that was building remote broadcast trucks for ESPN.

True 'SPNauts all: Sherry Simpson Petersen, husband Chris Petersen, ESPN romantics; and Getty Oil president Sid Petersen, Chris's dad. To Sid's left is Andy Brilliant, ESPN's first general counsel. Sherry's dad, Jim Simpson, renowned NBC and ESPN personality, likely took this Hollywood Bowl family celebration photo.

Now, the plot thickens, as Sherry remembers:

"You need to be back here in like five days or six days or something like that, we're going on the air, you know, you got to get back," we were told. My original plans were to go from interviewing back to Tarrytown just for the night because I was actually dating somebody in Tarrytown kind of.

Anyway, Chris goes, that's so dumb to drive back because we've got to find a place to live.

We should go out for dinner and celebrate getting jobs and you should just not go back to New York tonight. We should go out and celebrate. We needed to get an apartment, both not together.

And so he's like, well, just cancel. It doesn't make sense. Drive an hour and a half back, not an hour and a half. Back and down and then back up to find a place and then all the way back down to Maryland and all the way back up, you know, it totally made sense to stay.

So I called to say, sorry, I can't make it. I got the job offer. I'm going to stay up here and look for a place to live.

Chris goes, "What did he say?" And I said, "Oh, it's fine. It's like I told him." And Chris goes, "It wouldn't be fine if you canceled on a date on me," or something like that.

We found a Farmington home to share, and recruited Bruce Connal, as a third housemate, sharing a three-bedroom home.

So, that's how we met.

And, wouldn't you know it, in May of 1981 Chris and I married. I think we surprised a few. Not many people knew we were dating.

I was privy to the romance, though not sure Sherry knew that I knew. As an approachable marriage veteran, albeit at the time unsuccessfully, Chris would often ask the sort of guy-to-guy relationship questions of me. We definitely had a nice connection.

That Sherry, Chris, and Bruce found themselves sharing a home underlines the family connection this chapter is following.

Bruce, the son of Scotty Connal, was joined at ESPN by two of his sisters, Linda and Cathy, both of whom continue the family television legacy today. CEO Chet Simmons's son Jed, was an 'SPNaut unpaid intern.

Tragically, Bruce and Chris passed much too early for the promise their talents predicted.

While the hookup legacy of ESPN's early players is not without legend, true romance flowered.

Bob Waller, the magnificent voice of early *SportsCenter* anchoring, kept his romance with my friend Mary Walton on the hush-hush. So much so that I tried fixing him up with another friend, which turned into a clubbing fiasco. They both smirked when inviting me to their nuptials, Annette Stavola attending Mary. Annette, as mentioned in chapter 7, is today married to Tim Leisure, an ESPN executive who joined the network in days well past its adolescence.

Another romance, Bob Scanlon and Tes Stetson, reached romance proportions well worth recounting. Tes, the face that launched a thousand *SportsCenter* highlights, was the subject of Bob Scanlon's "who in the world is that?" when he saw her.

Smitten but not shy, Bob asked Tes to dinner and before long, she became Tes Stetson Scanlon, I know to the chagrin of quite a few gentleman 'SPNauts.

Tes was a *SportsCenter* and programming asset, and Bob recalls NCAA whip-around production as his second favorite ESPN memory.

Bob recalls "ESPN changed both my life and sports TV." And elaborates, though I can see his smile as he writes:

First day, October 10, 1979. In the 16 years there I played a role in many events that revolutionized the presentation of sports on television but one event changed my life.

As a cable network, we were unbound by traditional television's program schedule restrictions.

We had immense freedom to try virtually anything. Our NCAA Basketball Championship coverage was the first to cut live to other games where we often were able to witness last-second "buzzer beater" endings. We were free to use popular music as themes, Van Halen's "Jump" and Phil Collins's "One More Night" for that coverage, and without royalty fees.

On July 11, 1982 (a day I was trying to leave for vacation) we carried the six-hour marathon Davis Cup match between John McEnroe and Mats Wilander.

In 1983, I made the decision to join an America's Cup sailing race live after calling and asking permission from the Providence, RI station that was originating coverage.

Bob and Tes Scanlon, then and later

Our ability to televise flag-to-flag coverage of auto racing was instrumental in the meteoric rise of NASCAR, IndyCar, and Formula 1 racing popularity.

Those experiences pale in comparison to that first day in October 1979 when I was introduced to Tes Stetson, a stunningly beautiful woman working with SportsCenter. *After our nine-hour day jobs we often worked together covering live programming on nights and weekends.*

Two years later, we were married. This year we celebrated our 42nd anniversary.

I often say, when asked, about my career or our marriage, I am the most fortunate guy, ever.

CHAPTER 14

Too Good to Miss

FROM THE SCHOOL OF BE CAREFUL WHAT YOU ASK FOR COMES THIS story from the prolific Tom Reilly, who from launch day to his eventual retirement as ESPN coordinating producer, has left his mark in many ways on the culture of the network.

From his collaboration with George Grande to develop the still-in-use highlights shot sheet format which translates video action into live words for the live anchors of *SportsCenter* comes this story of Tom's most surreal ESPN moment.

So, invoking editorial privilege, even though it occurs in the network's adolescent time, given it falls from the pen of a true 'SPNaut, I take heed in Tom Reilly's urging that it is an ESPN story too good to miss.

Hence:

The Most Surreal Moment of My Life

It was late September of 1980. SportsCenter *had been on the air for just over a year. We were starting to cover big events with ENG crews consisting of a reporter, a field producer, and a cameraman. Our management decided that the Ali-Holmes fight scheduled for October 2nd at Caesar's Palace was worthy of big-time status. It was billed as "The Last Hurrah." They sent our boxing guru, Sal Marchiano, along with myself and Jeff Israel to provide in-depth coverage during the week preceding the fight.*

The aging Ali was a big underdog. At 38 years old he was considered finished by most experts. The intrigue of mentor vs. former sparring partner was a good storyline, but the big focus became just how great Ali looked physically.

Tom Reilly

On Tuesday morning we shot Larry Holmes's workout including some great footage of him sparring. After the shoot on the way back to our rooms out by the pool, who do we run into? Angelo Dundee! Ali's trainer! Sal introduced us and of course starts picking his brain. My first impression was how nice a man he was. Evasive, but really nice. As we're chatting him up, Sal tells Dundee about the Holmes workout. "I bet the champ would love to see that huh?" Dundee smiled and said "Yeah, I bet he would." Just then Sal looks at me and we both nodded with the same thought in mind. "Angie, how about we make a trade for a one-on-one interview with the Champ?" He said he would go up and check, and meet us in the coffee shop with an answer. About 15 minutes later he comes back down and lo and behold, we had a date with Muhammad Ali that afternoon.

We went up to Ali's double suite, which was enormous and packed with his entourage including women, children, and the smell of a kitchen in full gear. We were shown where we would do the interview and dropped off the tripod, light, and camera. We followed Angelo into the biggest bedroom I have ever seen; and there was Muhammad Ali, lying in the biggest bed I have ever seen. He was talking to his physical trainer who had just given him a massage. Sal greeted the champ, who he knew from covering many of his fights including the "Thrilla in Manila" for ABC Sports. Jeff and I positioned his enormous TV near the bed. I was in awe to say the least. Jeff hooked up the recorder and we began playing back the Holmes sparring session. Ali was immediately excited to see what we had, and soon started a running commentary to Dundee. Just when I thought life couldn't get any cooler, it happened! Ali tore off his sheets and jumped out of bed in front of the TV! He was stark naked and dancing around like only he could! He was shadowboxing at Holmes and yelling "You're slow and open! Look, Angie I got this! Pop-pop-pop . . . Bam! Pop-pop-pop . . . Bam!" I looked at Sal and we both couldn't believe what was happening right before our eyes! Here was the most famous human being on earth, showing off his new physique with all his manhood flapping around! "It's my fight, Angie! Mine! Pop-pop-pop . . . Bam!" He then dove back into bed and pulled up the sheets and finished his rant. We were all absolutely shell-shocked. It was the most surreal moment of my life!

We set up the interview in the adjacent room. Ali took a shower and then sat down with Sal. Everything was going great until we heard a huge commotion in the hallway. The door burst open and in stumbles Bundini Brown, Ali's cornerman and confidant. He's completely shitfaced drunk, and falls on Sal trying to kiss him. Just when I thought I had seen it all, Ali rips off his mike and starts beating the crap out of him, dragging him out into the hall. Muhammad was furious, but to his credit, he came back and gave us a great interview. We were amazed at that, and everything we had just witnessed. We couldn't stop talking about it that night at dinner, and for quite a while thereafter. I've probably told that story about a hundred times in my life. It was just incredible!

We milked that interview on SportsCenter for the entire week. People took notice. We got a lot of notoriety for getting that one-on-one. Ali boasted all week. He looked like he was in great shape. He was bet down from a big underdog, to 2–1 by the end of the week. He fooled all of us. Holmes was pretty classy in his press conferences, but played up his role as the undefeated champ in a big way. They had a lot of history together. He acknowledged Ali not only as his mentor, but his meal ticket back in the day. The hype for the fight was real. Much more than it deserved.

The fight itself was so disappointing. Ali held his own in the first round, but Holmes dominated the rest of the way. It was sad seeing Ali take a beating after our false expectations. Dundee stopped it in the 11th round. He had nothing in the tank. We later found out that he had been on a diuretic to lose all that weight, and wasn't really in true boxing shape. After the fight, Holmes went up to Ali's suite and told him, "I love you, man. . . . You're the greatest man ever." Ali responded, "If you loved me, why'd you beat me up like that?" Holmes laughed but was crying at the same time.

Ali should never have fought again. But of course he did, losing a cringeworthy bout to Trevor Berbick that was barely sanctioned. Parkinsonism had already began to set in for the most iconic sports figure in history. It was a sad end to a legend, like no other. I was just lucky to catch a glimpse, like no other.

CHAPTER 15

A Privileged Pedestal

THERE'S A PEDESTAL I'VE ALWAYS PUT WRITERS ON . . . AND NOW I ARE one, goes the groaner.

Idolizing Samuel Clemens, who wrote on the pool table I kissed on the top floor of the mansion he built on the Nook Farm in Hartford, and nearing the close of this project I can't help but invoke his advisory: "I conceive that the right way to write a story for boys is to write so that it will not only interest boys but strongly interest any man who has ever been a boy. That immensely enlarges the audience."

SC obviously penned that one before Billie Jean should have stuffed a pair of tennis balls under Bobby Riggs's loudmouth shirt.

What pen ownership does allow is the holder to have a say, and so this will be a four-course sitting, beginning with:

PRODIGAL PRODUCER

If you're this far along in this collection and narrative, you've figured out that many exits from the network by the earliest 'SPNauts were not exactly happy.

Bill Rasmussen and I lasted a while longer than much of our pre-Getty crew. Bill eventually succumbed to the indignities attendant to many visionaries, shunted to paper shuffling and ribbon cutting by Darth Evey.

Days later, I answered an expected call. On the other end was Barry Black, who must have drawn the short straw. "It's over," Barry said. "There'll be a check waiting for you to pick up."

I poured another drink.

And just like that my dreams cum nightmares intensified. Self-infliction continued through a few phases—advertising reincarnation, marriages, and stumbles—and grace inspired sobriety now entering its 37th year, as I write this.

Though I can only speak to my experience, there was a signature moment during which a power higher than me performed an emotional ectomy on me.

Tenderly, I spent a long time, one day at a time, with my 11 Step Program, assiduously avoiding any contact with the media and advertising hells where I starred and burned.

Turning to the peace that I knew existed, I turned to golf, actually finding a job as an assistant pro, cleaning clubs, folding shirts, smiling when I didn't feel like it, and picking grass cuttings off the pro shop carpet.

I worked at Farmington Woods, in Avon, Connecticut, where a cadre of ESPN slingers had come to live and play. Rick Churchill was head pro there. He and I had history. Good history, and by this time, 1990, Rick knew these ESPN guys didn't know me. He obliged with quiet intros.

The Farmington Woods enclave was nicely populated. I met Kathy Ackerson, ESPN Promotions leader, and her producer hubby Scott who migrated to Fox Sports as Rupert Murdoch went all in to win an NFL football television bidding war. I met Norby Williamson, Lee Rosenblatt, and John Colby, the composer of *SportsCenter*'s indelible "DaDaDa, DaDaDa" musical stinger.

And, I met Mo Davenport. On the Farmington Woods practice tee where Mo and I spent learning times together, I learned of his upcoming supervisory role for the college basketball season.

Something made me blurt a question to Mo about his needs in assembling a team for the season, and offering to apply. He asked what sort of ideas I might have.

I remember distinctly saying "Nothing live!"

The stress of live TV can be enormous, and while I can't blame it, there certainly were times when my adrenaline rush got tempered with depressants.

So, I proposed a series of pre-produced halftime features that could fill the time between basketball halves, giving the on-air play-by-play and analyst announcers a breather.

Mo's eyebrow raised and suggested I offer some topics. So I did and then next thing you know, Rick Churchill had to look for another assistant, though the season was soon to end. Mo, now general manager and senior vice president at ESPN Audio, and then NCAA Basketball coordinating producer, introduced me to Dan Steir, a talented production manager.

Dan and I worked out a series of feature reports, and off I went, on my own to Big East and ACC gyms and locker rooms.

On the opening evening of basketball season, which eventually saw towel-biting Hall of Fame coach Jerry Tarkanian's Runnin' Rebels of the University of Nevada lose in a revenge game to another Hall of Fame coach, Mike Krzyzewski of Duke, I had my own Hall of Fame coach experience.

The 1991 season was to be the Naismith Basketball Hall of Fame's 100th anniversary, so the season-opening halftime feature was to celebrate the occasion. In writing and producing it, I recall recreating the duck-on-the-rock game James Naismith played as a kid and inserting the mind-wringing potential that basketball may very well have been called boxball, as legend has it that Naismith asked the YMCA gym attendant to find him a box to nail to the gym's overhanging balcony. Instead a peach basket appeared, and the rambunctious rugby players Naismith was trying to tame with an indoor wintertime sport became our first hoopsters.

During that research the Naismith Hall of Fame PR staff showed me a small film can, which contained what they thought might be the only film of James Naismith ever taken. I promised to convert it to videotape for them and did, adding it to the halftime piece as a closer to the 100th anniversary feature.

Striding proudly from ESPN's editing bowels with completed feature in hand, I climbed the stairs to the much expanded production area en route to Dan Steir for a pregame screening.

Mo Davenport
COURTESY ESPN

As I passed, none other than ESPN's brand-new on-air analyst Jim Valvano sat on the corner of a desk with a phone cradled to his ear. I doubt anyone else heard this, but I did.

I heard Hall of Fame coach Jim Valvano say: "Honey, I'm in heaven. I can watch a half-dozen games at the same time!"

Later Mo and Dan steered me to another story, one about NCAA devising an insurance policy that would protect collegiate superstars, and hopefully keep them from jumping to the NBA or NFL before finishing school.

I met with Ted Dipple and Bill Hubbard of American Specialty Underwriters (ASU), correspondent with Lloyd's of London syndicates. They were creating the NCAA insurance for star players.

Almost instantly Ted lit my entrepreneurial fires when he explained that he and Bill were building a business that could and would take risks on just about anything as long as they could get a decent feel for the odds.

That sounded a lot like gambling to me, and I guess all insurance boils down to that. I was hooked, produced my last ESPN feature for Dan and Mo, and left ESPN on my own terms, thanking Mo for the cleansing opportunity.

And off to ASU as its marketing counsel and Lloyd's for a whirlwind of creativity, gratefully closing an 'SPN door until these pages.

GOLF

The second best thing I love about golf is the smell of freshly mown grass I didn't have to mow.

The best thing I love about golf is how it has influenced my life in so many ways, and that surely includes the birthing of ESPN.

I can't remember not playing golf. I still have visions of catching my pop's soft sand wedges with my first baseball glove, then chipping them back to him.

When Bill Rasmussen was calling Hartford Whalers play-by-play action, I inserted myself into his consciousness right away by stopping by the broadcast perch during breaks, at first introducing myself and then passing compliments.

We found out we were kindred spirits, media entrepreneurs at heart, sports lovers and conveniently for me, golfers. I invited Bill to play at the Donald Ross–designed gem, and A. W. Tilllinghast–reconstructed Wampanoag Country Club where I held a junior membership. We competed as partners in member-guest events. There I introduced Bill to J. R. Burrill, my golfing and pen-slinging mentor.

Jack's mentor was Tommy Armour. Good enough for me and superglued into my memory bank while browsing with Jack in the Winged Foot clubhouse where Armour was a famous member. When we came upon Armour's iconic photo of him lounging on a golf bench clad in his impeccable cardigan and undoubtedly cashmere sweater, Jack mused: "I think I still have that sweater in my closet."

I repeat that story to set up the partnering of Jack and Bill as PGA Tour commentators, as I had acquired broadcast rights to the Sammy Davis Greater Hartford Open.

The producer in my blood knew Bill's chatty optimism would fill the dead air Jack might have as he threaded a sentence through his colander that was sure to end up as either poetry or prophecy. They were a hit, and continued for a couple of Sammy Davis GHOs.

During the summer of ESPN's birthing, I tried to double-dip, through involvement with the WRCH tournament updates. Bill couldn't so the radio station's Pete Bliss rode shotgun for Jack.

Afterward I retired to the Hotel Sonesta bar, where I recognized and then sidled up to CBS's legendary golf producer Frank Chirkinian, who was enjoying as many see-thrus as I, and finally we began to chat.

I told Chirkinian about ESPN and surprisingly to me he already knew about it and wanted to know more, so he invited me to what I considered auditing a masterclass, observing his colorful producing from the innards of the CBS control room trailer.

It wasn't the last time "Ayatollah" Chirkinian and I had a close personal connection.

Years later at Augusta Country Club during Master's week, we met while I was producing infomercial takes of then sober Pat Summerall for a client.

My home in Naples, Florida, had given me the opportunity to renew a previous contact with Ken Venturi, the third of CBS's golf Mount Rushmore. He lived in nearby Marco Island, where I had a hotel client that I got Ken to visit frequently, on the cuff.

Years earlier when Venturi sued jeweler giant Bill Savitt for annually using Venturi's image holding the grandiose diamond-studded putter, we had shared personal lawyer Ed Daly, who recruited my expertise as an ad exec to testify to the potential value that Savitt had not paid Venturi.

As court sessions go, there was interminable wait time and interruptions, giving Venturi and I plenty of time to get to know each other and our habits. Wouldn't you know there was a pub a driver and a wedge away from the court. We became good friends.

Chirkinian and Summerall were concerned with Venturi's continuing penchant for imbibing, so much so they asked me to see if Ken would entertain a visit. Over dinner I tried to obliquely mention to Ken that I'd been with his pals and they were thinking about a trip to Southwest Florida and would like to get together.

"You tell them there will be no intervention here, and they should stay away," insisted the winner of the 1964 US Open, who muted youthful stuttering to become the icy cool voice that has set a standard for golf commentary.

LAS VEGAS AND BOB MURPHY

Golf also played a big role in the mega schmoozing we put on in our debut at the National Cable Television Association trade show.

I relied on Harold Post's Design Workshop to build a booth the NCTA put in an aisle where Ted Turner and his nascent CNN shared space with our Satcom 1 satellite partner WTBS.

Bob Chamberlain was charged with a Las Vegas Hilton hospitality suite where PGA Tour winner Bob Murphy autographed and drank with the best of us, Stu Evey and me leading the way.

Long before today's geometry and physics enhanced ball speed and torsion measuring obsession, Murphy advised me to just tee it high and let it fly. The next morning he put a dozen or more of his customized long tees in my early morning shaky hand.

Bob was to entertain cable VIPs we invited to an early morning fun golf event. I was his cart driver, and Bob was to play one hole with each of the foursomes that we entertained at Del Webb's Sahara-Nevada Country Club.

Halfway down the first hole, Bob turned to look in the carry-all space of the golf cart and then quickly at me, he pealed: "Peter, where's the beer?" A quick turnaround ensued.

A day later, exhausted, I staggered back to the convention hall to visit our booth, taking a moment to slide over to meet Ted Turner who had appeared at his WTBS/CNN booth.

There was a real moment of ingratiation when, shaking hands, I mentioned I was already drinking at Newport's Black Pearl when he docked there after winning the America's Cup in 1977 to celebrate with his crew.

His all-news network and our all-sports network were about to change television forever and we knew it, and between us we made a bet who would get on the air first.

When his RCA Satcom III commercial communications satellite, the reserved home for CNN, got lost in space, he defaulted and moot was the wager, but weeks after NASA owned up to the big boo-boo, a signed Ben Franklin arrived in the mail.

To say our debut at the NCTA was successful is an understatement. Shortly thereafter Bill appeared on the cover of NCTA's *CableVision* magazine.

GETTY, GOLF, AND HOLLYWOOD

When we packed up our Las Vegas cable convention, our crew went in all directions. Bill, Lou, and I were drawn by Stu Evey to meet the Getty folks who were making the ESPN dream and birth happen.

Three indelible moments occurred in the visit.

The first was a big conference room meeting where Getty brass were introduced to us. Sid Petersen, then Getty president, I recall startlingly advised us that there was enough money at Getty to buy NBC, ABC, and CBS combined and Getty did not want to be embarrassed by this new venture: what I read then as a wholehearted endorsement, which was later seconded when his son Chris became an 'SPNaut, and a frequent lunching friend during our early times.

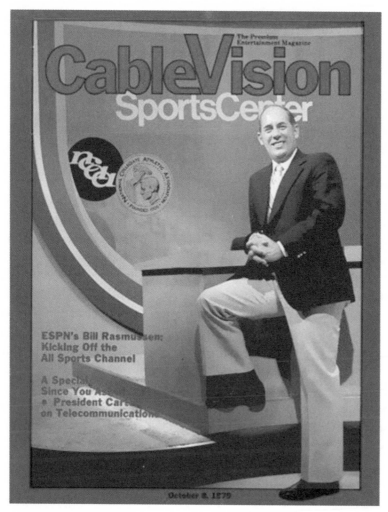

Bill on the cover of *CableVision*
COURTESY BILL RASMUSSEN

Later, Michael Freeman, in his book, tempers Petersen differently, telling his board members "I think we can make money on this network, if not we can cut it off at $35 million and write it off as drilling a bad hole."

Golf was the second, with the Getty biggies at Wilshire Country Club under the jaw-dropping HOLLYWOOD sign. Of course golf was preceded by a wet lunch, again Evey and I overachieving.

Golf was followed by mandatory visit to the amazing Getty Museum and Rembrandt, Renoir, Van Gogh, Monet, et al. I was drawn to the incredible early photography collection there.

Later, after mentioning the Brown Derby to Stu Evey, he insisted that he and I do a get-to-know-each-other-better separate visit to the celebrity watering hole, a third blurry but indelible memory. We entered the famous hangout and he was greeted as a friend would be. Perhaps a little too arrogant to be starstruck, I was mostly trying to figure out who the familiar faces I kept seeing were. There were no leading men or ladies browning out that evening.

Stu and I browned out, all right, and I can't recall which of us needed to wrap an arm around the unsteady other, but interlocked and unsteady we were, thankfully driven to the feathers that would nurse the oncoming inevitable.

The next time I would see Stu Evey was the evening we launched ESPN and I saw the chair with "Stu Evey Executive Producer" splashed across the back.

False pride swirled me toward the outer edges of a whirlpool pulling me elsewhere, mostly downward, but not before golf and I made a contribution I continue to hold quietly as a positive memory.

USGA, BALTUSROL, AND FRANK HANNIGAN

Not long after Andy North sank his final putt to win the 1978 US Open, Jack Burrill, who by then had nurtured an interest in golf broadcasting, suggested we see if we could get similar radio rights to broadcast the 1979 edition and syndicate it.

It was to be staged at Baltusrol, nearby in northern New Jersey and easy to manage, we thought without big travel costs. Jack was a Connecticut Golf Association board member and had access to the United States Golf Association decision-makers.

So, he made an appointment, and off we went to USGA HQ in Far Hills, New Jersey.

That day we met with John Laughheimer and Frank Hannigan, USGA bishops in the Golf House sanctuary library. Its walls are lined from floor to ceiling with books of printed golf decisions, USGA official interpretations of golf rules made since 1894.

In the interceding time Bill's vision for ESPN had not only whet my appetite, but Jack's as well, so we both refocused.

Months later, along came an invite to actually play a round of golf on the famous golf enclave carved from the farmland of Baltus Roll by equally renowned A. W. Tillinghast.

It was the site and the day of my most embarrassing golf moment.

When my tee time came, it graciously ended up being witnessed by Bob Ross, Baltusrol's golf professional who had friended me because we shared early golf roots at Groton, Connecticut's Shennecossett golfing grounds.

Though I'd calmed my nerves earlier with swing oil, my fingers were shaking when I put the Bob Murphy elongated tee into the ground.

One gulp and a club waggle and somehow my backswing lurched off the ground, milliseconds later digging up the biggest, baddest, fattest divot surely anyone has ever taken on the historic first tee of Baltusrol. It must have weighed a pound as my caddie retrieved and replaced it, with loving care and precision.

I couldn't look at Jack, or Bob. And couldn't think of anything else for the duration of a mortifyingly badly played round of golf on that historic A. W. Tillinghast layout.

Here Come the Cops

So with one of my sons, Patrick, a golf fan himself in tow, a caravan of us that included Jack's son Jason, too, headed to Baltusrol to cover the 1980 US Open. I say a caravan, because we'd figured out a work-around from the restrictive credentials Hannigan had given us.

We were not allowed to broadcast live at any time from the golf course.

ABC had on-course live rights. They were not part of the ESPN family yet. Our credentials let us record to tape. So we did.

We ripped the tape out of cameras and tossed it with some make-shift notes to drivers like Jason, who'd race the 127 miles from there to Bristol ESPN studios, making highlights available three hours after we'd record them.

The tape racing shuttle continued for the four-day duration of the Jack Nicklaus shot-for-shot duel with Japan's Isao Aoki.

Patrick reminds me every US Open Sunday, always on Fathers' Day, of the perch he had aside Baltusrol's 18th hole where Nicklaus holed a 12-foot birdie putt to ensure his victory.

While sports broadcasters and producers are not supposed to root for anyone, I know that Lou Palmer and I were rooting for Nicklaus, who made a special effort to be with us every day after his press conferences. Jack had seen the ESPN logo on our camera and actually sought us out after the first round. He explained to Lou that he'd been watching ESPN ever since we launched. His cable company was one of our early carriers. Nicklaus instructed Lou to meet him every day, just outside the press tent, and he'd have a word for our cameras.

You can bet your sweet bippy we were rooting for Jack.

Baltusrol coverage nearly got my overripe creative ideas to put our crew in the clink. Aching to make out of the ordinary and interesting stories to feed the *SportsCenter* team, I'm afraid I pushed our New Jersey crew a bit.

We made predawn shoots of USGA setting up the golf course, and testing green speeds with stimpmeters, but it was a late-night shoot that brought the cops.

We were breaking into a cemetery. Earlier when I scouted the grave of Baltus Roll, who'd been robbed and murdered by bad guys who knew Baltus was flush from selling a string of horses, the cemetery was open.

Figuring it would make for a spooky atmosphere to tell the Baltus story, I'd set the shoot for after dark, at graveside. It was locked. Not to be deterred, while testing the fencing for scalability, a searchlight invaded our space.

Sure enough, it was the cops, and they were having a time believing me, until I brought them back to the crew area so I could show them cameras and portable lights we'd begun to lift and lower over the fence.

We got off. I got laughed at.

Frank Hannigan Makes History with ESPN

Weeks later Frank Hannigan wrote me a letter. It was a classic, hand typed on onion-skin stationery with a carbon copy. He mailed it to me asking me to pass the copy along to Chet Simmons.

In it Frank said he was on his way to be with peers of the R&A, more formally, Royal and Ancient Trust Company, which governs golf worldwide and yearly stages The Open on famous British soil.

He thought he might be able to talk R&A and BBC television bishops into allowing ESPN to take the BBC feed on Thursday and Friday of upcoming Open competitions, if we were interested.

There was a catch, Frank wrote, as Chet and I drooled. Frank wanted to be an on-air commentator if the deal materialized. It did and he was.

Frank Hannigan went on to a great on-air golf career and a six-year stint as executive director of the USGA. ESPN went on to televise weekday golf regularly.

And long before I went on to write golf books, films, and the like, my favorite contribution to the game that influenced my life in so many ways is having a small part in bringing weekday televised tournament play to hungry American golf fans long before it begat another 24/7 cable offspring.

Getting legit via golf has always been a strength, learned by shadowing Jack, and as ESPN grew we'd double-team some of the newbies, Jack always hoping he'd score a role as a golf commentator via my connection.

Sadly it didn't happen, though it should have. His magical turn of a phrase would have been a pure antidote to Boomer's genius highlight narratives.

As it stood, we enjoyed making **Rich Caulfield**'s acquaintance, spending moments traipsing around the 18 stations of the course at nearby Pine Valley, so close to ESPN and easy to slip away for a golf round. Rich like many a rookie to sports television eventually became ESPN's outdoor life maven, working the hunting and fishing audiences.

A Fox Foursome

The rage to succeed that burned in this sports soul was rudely awakened mostly by stature, skill, and a stubborn romance with words.

It has always been clear to me that sitting in the free lunch press box is delightfully more comfortable than warming a bench after a gut-busting week of practice.

My competitor's ember, assuaged by YMCA hoops, slow-pitch softball, and always golf as vocation and hobby, continued to glow until well after the dreaded AARP card arrived.

That DNA mixed media and sports with mom Betsey's beauty of poetry to produce eyebrow-lifting Irish triplets, John Patrick and his twin brothers Matthew Adam and Douglas Owen.

In a first home, protecting my and Betsey's sanity, the windows in one room were boarded, with an anything goes rule in the confines of that room: Wiffle ball, plastic golf, and general rambunctious tomfoolery was allowed.

It was inevitable the Fox boys would be addicted to sports. Our family's ESPN connection was high-quality sports dope. Juggling an incredible commuting schedule to see all three on the same Little League team too infrequently for all of us resulted in a joy not many dads had to brag about. On a best day, Pat would catch, Matt would pitch, and Doug would gobble up balls in center field. The parts were interchangeable, and the Fox boys were something to see and brag on.

Whirring forward to those ESPN birthing times, in many ways four Fox boys, three young and one maturity restricted, were part of this courtside, pitch-side press box and greenside access that, I've confirmed, have survived the decades as moments to savor.

Our two-on-two pickup games on famous basketball courts while ESPN production crews were setting up are experiences most pops and progeny don't share. We did and do and are grateful.

Spending innings in the Fenway Park broadcast booth while Ken Coleman and Joe Castiglione called the game and chewing the fat with Ted Williams, thanks to an invite Lou Palmer arranged for us, are Red Sox priceless memory jewels.

Inside the ropes Greater Hartford Open family passes to witness John Mahaffey snap at Pop, whose tee shot almost hit John's wife in the gallery, remain heirlooms of embarrassment.

Patrick's greenside tree climb at Baltusrol in 1980 to witness Jack Nicklaus's Father's Day US Open victory there is an image I'll always remember.

Happy Endings

Some happy endings begin with being rubbed the wrong way.

To say that is how Stu Evey of Getty Oil and I got on isn't exaggeration.

While it is unfair to diss a guy after he's gone, Stu earned it, and he took his shots at me. I recount the preliminaries because the final act is a happy ending.

Throughout this missive, you may have picked up allusions to Evey's bullish ways that ultimately sent me reeling. They did not escape the purview of other 'SPNauts.

Evey's right hand, George Conner, has much great to say about his boss, but recognizes "Stu was controversial in many ways. He alienated a lot of people."

Chet Simmons is said to have called Evey a "jock sniffer," according to multiple members of his NBC-expatriated inner circle who'd meet nightly for beers and bullshit at the Farmington Inn hotel that became their barracks before headquarters was built.

Founder Bill Rasmussen tells the story of how Stu in no uncertain terms made him a benchwarmer, telling him that Simmons was in charge and Rasmussen was to "Stay out of his way."

I knew Stu Evey the day we met. I read it in his eyes. We confirmed it later as I'd discussed elsewhere in our bourbon bout at the Brown Derby.

We shared more than an affinity for 80 proof; he didn't miss a short skirt or a well-turned ankle.

Simmons would describe his nightclubbing with Evey as whoring for dollars, calling the New York City sessions with Evey as drinks and winks.

During our mirrored street urchin days, Stu and I learned the ways and means of the pool hall hustle. That kind of education can lead a guy to some ugly career steps.

Earlier reference to Stu as Getty Oil's fixer version of Ray Donovan is certified in his *Creating an Empire* confession, "Not everything I did was pretty. In fact, some of the tasks were downright ugly."

Politics was my ugly. There is much wisdom in the allegory about watching sausage being made; it is akin to the legislative process. Crippling the truth is more like it.

So around life's carousel Stu Evey and I rode different horses, and bumped into each other on the way to Betty Ford. In moments of sobriety Stu Evey and I shared with Betty Ford, our happy endings make the consternation of business seem so small in the full bloom of recovery.

Betty Ford and Peter Fox

Stu writes of his addiction being lifted at the Betty Ford Institute, being triggered by a memory of a J. Paul Getty anecdote with him, saying in *Creating an Empire*:

"I had an invitingly inexplicable feeling inside. It was an epiphany and I simply knew it would be easy to quit. But it hit me then—like an uppercut to the gut that lifts you off the ground—and to this day never have I had the occasion in the 19 years since to ever want to have a drink again. It was a bolt of lightning to my soul."

Stu Evey died on December 8, 2017, a free man. I wish I had known. The sarsparilla we could have shared would have been drunk gratefully.

As it is we share the grace of recovery with Betty Ford, Stu at her institute and me at the Broadcaster of the Year awards a few years later.

Our sharing of Betty Ford came after I'd been graduated from an East Coast version of celebrity rehab in Newport, but very much like Stu, a lightning bolt seemed to strike there on my birthday in 1987.

At Edge Hill's daily group the leader slipped a cassette into a boombox and played Lennon and McCartney's "In My Life."

When the words of the refrain played, I wretched and sobbed uncontrollably, leaping out of my chair to leave the group room.

After a while I composed myself, somehow and returned to the room.

The lifting resembled Stu's, and nary a sip have crossed these lips since. I believe in that miracle.

When next we meet, I'm challenging Stu to a game of nine-ball for bragging rights.

What Does the Future Hold?

The New Art of Prompting

Somehow a street urchin smokin' Pall Malls and cleaning the felt in a three-table pool hall ended up with a little more than a nodding acquaintance with Google Cloud's chief technology officer.

Ever since Will Grannis and I ended up advising a mutual business friend, I've appreciated a twinkle he sports, hinting at a mischievous chapter in his history. It belies his powerhouse brain.

When media barged artificial intelligence into our consciousness, I somehow knew he'd be part of that action. Sure enough, as I was ruminating on the subject a social media trough spilled an article by Will on a home page I visit.

Jumping out of his brainbender *AI as the Next Computing Platform* was the phrase "who was skilled in the new art of prompting."

It keyed AI success to the new art of prompting. I was gifted with the old art of prompting by my city editor during copyboy times.

"Ask one good question. Shut up. And when you hear a silence, ask how," he taught.

While satellites, digits, and engineers have fueled a great trip on the media whirlwind for me, the prospect of a technology that could write scared the shit out of me.

That is until I asked how?

So, yes it writes. Not very well yet, but it will, he judged. As a tool, it means better and faster, now.

For a guy who used to give flowers to the local librarian so I could call the reference desk rather than traipse across town, AI looked to be

Google on steroids, and sure enough along came Will and friends, with Bard, their AI chat service.

So, in a forward attempt by a Jimmy Olsen turned 'SPNaut to anticipate an AI-lit sports revolution that might exceed the one celebrated in this book, I spent some time trying to think up a good question, asked Bard, and when it got quiet, asked how.

In this age of expanding artificial intelligence, what will become of sports cable television and how will sports fans be entertained and informed?
Artificial intelligence (AI) is rapidly changing the way we consume media, and sports is no exception. Here are some ways that AI is likely to impact the future of sports cable television:

- *Personalized recommendations*: AI can be used to recommend sports content to viewers based on their interests, viewing history, and social media activity. This will make it easier for fans to find the content they want to watch, without having to scroll through endless channels or search through menus.

- *Enhanced analytics*: AI can be used to provide more in-depth analysis of sports games and events. This could include things like real-time player tracking, predictive analytics, and historical insights. This will help fans better understand the game and make more informed predictions.

- *Virtual reality (VR) and augmented reality (AR)*: AI can be used to create immersive VR and AR experiences for sports fans. This could allow fans to feel like they are actually at the game, or to get a behind-the-scenes look at the action.

- *Interactive features*: AI can be used to create interactive features for sports fans. This could include things like polls, quizzes, and games. This will help fans engage with the content and make it more fun to watch.

- *Automated production*: AI can be used to automate many of the tasks involved in producing sports broadcasts. This could free up human resources to focus on more creative and strategic aspects of the production.

Overall, AI is likely to make sports cable television more personalized, informative, and engaging. This will help sports fans stay connected with their favorite teams and players, and make the viewing experience more enjoyable.

In addition to the above, here are some other ways that sports fans may be entertained and informed in the future.

- *Through social media*: Social media platforms like Twitter and Facebook are already being used by sports fans to follow their favorite teams, players, and leagues. In the future, AI could be used to make social media even more engaging for sports fans. For example, AI could be used to recommend relevant content to fans, or to generate personalized highlight reels.

- *Through mobile apps*: Mobile apps are another way that sports fans are already getting their news and information. In the future, AI could be used to make mobile apps even more useful for sports fans. For example, AI could be used to provide real-time game updates, or to help fans find the best deals on tickets and merchandise.

- *Through virtual reality and augmented reality*: As VR and AR technology continues to develop, it is likely to become more common in sports broadcasting. This could allow fans to experience sports games in a whole new way. For example, VR could be used to put fans in the stands or on the field, or AR could be used to overlay statistics and information on the game.

The future of sports cable television is still uncertain, but it is clear that AI is playing a growing role. As AI technology continues to develop, it is likely to have a major impact on the way we consume sports media.

How will virtual and augmented reality create feelings that the fans are actually at the game and getting a behind the scenes look at the action?

Virtual reality (VR) and augmented reality (AR) are two technologies that are rapidly evolving and have the potential to revolutionize the way we experience sports. VR can create an immersive experience that allows users to feel like they are actually at the game, while AR can overlay digital information onto the real world, providing users with a behind-the-scenes look at the action.

Here are some specific ways that VR and AR can be used to create feelings that the fans are actually at the game and getting behind the scenes look at the action:

- *VR*: VR headsets can be used to transport fans to the stadium or arena, where they can see the game from any seat in the house. They can also be used to provide fans with a 360-degree view of the action, allowing them to see everything that's happening on the field or court.
- *AR*: AR glasses or smartphones can be used to overlay digital information onto the real world, such as statistics, player stats, or even replays of the action. This can give fans a deeper understanding of the game and help them make more informed predictions.
- *Mixed reality*: Mixed reality is a combination of VR and AR, which allows users to interact with digital content in the real world. This could be used to create interactive experiences for fans, such as allowing them to control the game or play games with their favorite players.

These are just a few of the ways that VR and AR can be used to enhance the sports fan experience. As these technologies continue to develop, it is likely that we will see even more innovative and immersive ways to use them to watch sports.

In addition to the above, here are some other ways that VR and AR can be used in sports:

- *Training and simulation:* VR and AR can be used to train athletes and simulate game scenarios. This can help athletes improve their skills and prepare for competition.
- *Coaching and analysis:* VR and AR can be used to provide coaches with insights into their players' performance. This can help coaches make better decisions about training and strategy.

- *Broadcasting*: VR and AR can be used to create more immersive and engaging broadcasts for fans. This could include things like putting fans in the stands or on the field, or providing behind-the-scenes looks at the action.

- *Marketing and advertising*: VR and AR can be used to create more engaging and interactive marketing and advertising campaigns for sports teams and leagues.

The possibilities for using VR and AR in sports are endless. As these technologies continue to develop, we are likely to see even more innovative and creative ways to use them to enhance the sports fan experience.

What sort of interactive features during a baseball game, for example, can a fan expect to come from AI in the future?

Here are some interactive features during a baseball game that fans can expect to come from AI in the future.

- *Real-time player tracking*: AI can be used to track the movements of players in real time. This information can be used to create interactive features that allow fans to see how players are positioned on the field, or to predict where they are likely to go next.

- *Predictive analytics*: AI can be used to analyze game data and predict future outcomes. This information can be used to create interactive features that allow fans to make bets on the game, or to see how different strategies might affect the outcome.

- *Virtual reality (VR) and augmented reality (AR)*: VR and AR can be used to create immersive experiences that allow fans to feel like they are actually at the game. This could include things like putting fans in the stands or on the field, or providing behind-the-scenes looks at the action.

- *Interactive games and quizzes*: AI can be used to create interactive games and quizzes that allow fans to test their knowledge of the game. This could be a fun way for fans to learn more about baseball and to interact with each other.

- *Social media integration*: AI can be used to integrate social media into the game experience. This could allow fans to interact with each other and with the game in real time, or to share their thoughts and reactions with the world.

These are just a few of the interactive features that fans can expect to see from AI in the future of baseball. As AI technology continues to develop, we are likely to see even more innovative and creative ways to use it to enhance the fan experience.

Here are some specific examples of how AI is being used in baseball today:

- The MLB Statcast system uses AI to track the movements of players and balls in real time. This information is used to provide fans with detailed statistics and insights about the game.
- The Statcast VR app uses VR to allow fans to experience the game from the perspective of a player or umpire.
- The MLB Ballpark app uses AR to overlay statistics and information on the game.
- The MLB At Bat app uses AI to recommend relevant content to fans, such as news stories, highlights, and fantasy baseball projections.

These are just a few examples of how AI is being used in baseball today. As AI technology continues to develop, we are likely to see even more innovative and creative ways to use it to enhance the fan experience.

When ESPN was founded satellite and cable television were in their infancy, much like AI is today, at least in terms of market acceptance, so how is a next technological advancement going to threaten AI, like streaming has done to cable?

It is difficult to say for sure what the next technological advancement will be that will threaten AI, but here are a few possibilities:

- *Quantum computing*: Quantum computing is a new type of computing that is much more powerful than traditional computers. It is still in its early stages of development, but it has the potential to revolutionize many industries, including AI.

- *Brain-computer interfaces (BCIs)*: BCIs are devices that allow humans to control computers with their minds. They are still in their early stages of development, but they have the potential to make AI more accessible and user-friendly.

- *Artificial general intelligence (AGI)*: AGI is a hypothetical type of AI that would be as intelligent as a human being. It is still a long way off, but if it is ever achieved, it could pose a serious threat to AI.

- *Existential risk from artificial intelligence*: This is a hypothetical scenario in which AI becomes so powerful that it poses a threat to humanity. It is a very complex and controversial topic, but it is one that is worth considering as AI continues to develop.

It is also possible that AI will not be threatened by any single technological advancement, but rather by a combination of factors. For example, the development of quantum computing and BCIs could make it possible to create AI that is more powerful and user-friendly than ever before. This could lead to a widespread adoption of AI, which could in turn pose a threat to human jobs and even our way of life.

Only time will tell what the future holds for AI. However, it is important to be aware of the potential threats that it poses, so that we can take steps to mitigate them.

So if Z is your generation, and ESPN and Bard are still around, see if the above comes to pass and give a shout-out to both from the 'SPNauts. My brain hurts. I'm out.

Acknowledgments

In the struggle to shut the lid on this project, I find myself in a dreaded cramping position and relegated to finding words to define closure falling from the pen of someone else.

Dickens has never been a favorite of mine, scaring the shit out of kids at Christmastime, regaling the conversion of a grouchy old skinflint with ghosts. I fully expect when assigned a report on his *Tale of Two Cities*, I used classic comic books to get the gist and spin some sort of yarn that would pass grading muster. And yet, here I am, cramped to put to phrase the words that thank the people who have championed the writing of the early ESPN travails and triumphs.

So, CD, I beg your indulgence because you said it well, and for me: *"It was the best of times, it was the worst of times, it was the age of wisdom, it was the age of foolishness. . . ."*

The months of reflection, recollection, regaling, and recapturing the spiritual combination of faith and failings that accompanied the disruptive birthing of ESPN have run the spectrum of emotions.

So, where do the thanks begin?

I think most of all with my children, Pat, Matt, and Doug, who while they may have experienced some ESPN-related highs, deserved so much more that a purpose-driven Pop usurped.

I need to thank their mom, Betsey, too, for the special sort of familial glue she brandished during the worst of times.

Then there's the lengthy list of siblings, Cy, Meredith, Deb, Bobbi, Betsy, Nancy, and Mike, who freed me to pursue flops and fancy flights in the age of foolishness and beyond.

Without a cast of hundreds in recovery this and years of other good work would never have happened. You know who you are.

Now, I come to the special ESPN friends who encouraged this project. Bill Rasmussen leads the pack but is followed closely by Mary Walton and Dennis Randall.

Super contributors like George Conner, Tom Reilly, Bill Shanahan, the Chrises Berman and LaPlaca, Bob Ley, Sherry Simpson, Annette Stavola, Mike Soltys, Geoff Bray, Chuck Pagano, Phil Kulas, Ellen Beckwith, and Ken Boudreau have my full-throated appreciation, in what turns out to be our best of times age.

Regarding Dickens's age of wisdom, I must have been at the airport when that ship came in. But now in a fourth decade of "wisdom to know the difference" incantations, I have accrued enough smarts to know who I owe big time.

They are my two besties, a unique pair that I love who have never seen me drink alcohol. I'm married to bestie one, Gwen Conley. Her songs breathe life into me daily. Her heart is bigger than her talents. Her standards demand growth. Her support guarantees it.

I partner with bestie two, Dr. James A. Trainham III. A friend, client, buddy, student, and supporter supreme, Dr. Trainham's friendship means as much to me as his scientific contributions to this world should to you.

Leaving my one last question:

What's next?